Shamanic Energy Medicine

Poetic Messages of Healing Wisdom

*Healing Journeys Through Ancient
Wisdom, Forgiveness & Love*

A Divine Heretic Book

by
Janine Palmer (Silver Moon) CHT

Copyright © 2018 by Janine Palmer (Silver Moon) CHT

All rights reserved. No part of this publication may be reproduced, distributed, or transmitted in any form or by any means, including photocopying, recording, or other electronic or mechanical methods, without the prior written permission of the author, except in the case of brief quotations embodied in critical reviews and certain other noncommercial uses permitted by copyright law.

Wolf with ethnic leaves image designed by 0melapics / Freepik.

Printed in the United States of America

ISBN 13: Paperback: 978-1-948172-45-5
eBook: 978-1-948172-44-8

Library of Congress Control Number: 2018940393

STONEWALL PRESS
PAVING YOUR WAY TO SUCCESS

Stonewall Press
363 Paladium Court
Owings Mills, MD 21117
www.stonewallpress.com
1-888-334-0980

Other books by Janine Palmer

MAIN BOOKS:
Divine Heretic – Standing Holy
Divine Heretic – In Christ Consciousness
Divine Heretic – Sacred Scribe
Divine Heretic – Mystical Fire
Divine Heretic – Alchemist
Divine Heretic – Hierophant
Divine Heretic – Hidden Keys

GENRE SPECIFIC BOOKS
(Material Pulled from Main Books)
Energy Healing Wisdom – Poetic Messages
Spiritual Healing Wisdom – Poetic Messages
Divine Healing Wisdom – Poetic Messages
Rising Above Dogma – Poetic Reflection
For Romance – Poetic Tales & Story Poems
Heart Speak – Poetic Tales & Story Poems
Book of Worthiness – Modern Day Gospel of Good News
Apocalypse of Worthiness – Modern Day Gospel of Good News

This book is dedicated to my family with deep love and to all the people who inspired me to write and to all poets and writers. The poetry contained herein is an acknowledgement to the healing powers of writing. Writing about the importance of processing and releasing emotions becomes artistic expression. Energy needs to flow. These tales are about releasing those blocks. Trust the process of unfolding and spiritual evolvement.

Blessings, love and light.
Janine Palmer (Silver Moon) CHT

Table of Contents

Foreword xv

Sacred Temple

Darkness and Silence 2
Capstone 4
Your Temple 6
Sanctity – The Woods 7
The Druid Tree 8
Monastery 10
Mysterious Gate 11

Glimpses of Soul

Divine Flame 14
Our Goddess 15
Echoes of the Soul 16
Hold Space 18
Mists of Spirit 19
The Magic of the Soul 20
White Thorn 21
Little Fields 23

Mystery & Grace

Dancing Flame 26
My Light 28
The Surface 30
Tresses 32
Open to the Gifts 34
White Wolf 36

Mystical & Sacred

The Eagle and the Raven 38
Walking Between Worlds 39
Experiences 41
Forces 42
The Tree at Twilight 43
The Raven's Call 44
On Her Journey 45

Divine Wisdom & Energy

Medicine Speaks 48
Turn the Page 49
Branches of Moonlight 51
Teacher 55
Their Healing 57
Living Prayer 58
Wisdom Keepers 60
What We Learn 62
Your Keys of Sacred Light 63
Tempo 65

Transformative Fire

Trial by Fire 68
Resurrected 69
The Ashes 70
Dragon's Fire 72
Frozen Heart, Blade of Fire 74
The Stake 77
Seek Among the Ashes 80

Forms of Healing & Forgiveness

Nature's Breath 84
Open to the Gifts 86
Snares 88
Well of Forgiveness 89
Your Cure 90

The Flower and Her Power 91
Clean Slate 93
Go Into it 95
Smoke 97
The Doctor 99
Ancestor's Inner Warrior 100
Ancestor's Pain – Ghosts and Bones 102
Collective Healing 106
From the Spirit 108

Ascension & Spiritual Alchemy

Crumbling Falsehoods 110
The Sword 112
Sacred Breeze 114
Pieces of Her Soul 116
It's Only a Test 118
Higher Self & The Dream 119
Meet Me 121
Spiral 123
Drum Beat 125

Your Magnificence & Worthiness

Gatekeeper 128
Ultimate Oblivion 129
Whispers and Shadows 131
The Lamps 133
Find Peace in Love 135
Ropes 137
Love Now Hidden 139
Flowers or Weeds 140

Blessed Be Our Magic

Do You Feel Nature? 144
Nature's Beauty Speaks 145
Dancing Shadows 146
Thanks and Blessings 148

Through the Trees 150
In the Company of the Trees 151
Trees and Stones 153
Feathers 154
Under the Wolf Moon 155
Fully Blessed 157
The Breath of Love 158

Your Own Honor

Second Sight 162
In Gratitude and Release, the Rose 164
Star Gate 165
Rewrite Your Addiction 167
Detachment 169

Mirror, Mirror

Mirror of Forgiveness 172
Merlin's Beard 174
Remedy 175
Souls 177
Spirit Wind 178
Light 179
Any Hell 181
Tranquility 183
They Resurrect 185
Powerful and Pure 186
Needs Must 188

Shedding Skins & Shells

Hints and Clues 192
Bless 193
Ghosts 195
False Hell 197
Broken Glass 198
Dead Wood 200
The Trigger 201

Powerful Potion...203
Your Demon 205
Bloody Armor..207
Resentment 209

Initiations & Battle Scars

Traps 212
Treasure Beneath 214
Elixir or Poison? 216
Above & Beyond 218
Battles 219
Triggered Memories... 221
Spirit Guide 223
Kinks 225
Bygones 227
Tribes 229

Judgment & Ego

Ego Burns Our Wings 232
Fly...234
Side Show 235
The Warrior's Field 236
The Alpha Male & Female 238
The Deceiver... 240

The Suffering & Shadow

Shadows...242
Just Doing a Dance...243
Broken Sword 245
Place of Pain 248
Layers of Loss and Rust 250
A Reflection of Truth 252
Broken Sword 253
The Dark Tent 256
Unbending...258
The Suffering.. 260

The Grief..262

Illusion and the Veil

Death or Release 266
Tame the Ghosts 268
The Dark Will Test You.............................. 269
Hidden...270
The War 272

Beyond Masks & Disguise

Masks...276
Vortex of Destruction 278
His Mask... 280
Emotions & Memories... or Demons & Ghosts?.........282
Connections 284
Glow...287
When They Fall... 288

Light Through the Cracks

Druid Priest...292
Smokey Tendrils..295
Druid Tower Library 297
The Cross 299
The Bell... 301
Energy Vampire...303
Things Married 305
Our Own Love & Trust 307
Torrent.. 309
Tangled Threads... 310

Freedom Through Awakening

Clearly.. 314
Within or Without...................................... 316
Shadows from the Tree of Life.....................317
Poison Wine 318
Raven Wood 320
The Awakening...322

Soul Song 323
Sleeping Beauty Awakened and Rising 325

Into Knowing, Beyond Belief

Death Rattle 328
Song of the Divine 330
To Question, To Seek 331
Iron Stone 333
Whispers of Destiny 335
Power to Heal 336
By Choice 338

Metaphors & Deeper Truth

Dragon's Fang 340
Motion 343
Windows and Doors 344
Karma 346
Your Father's Armor 348
Balance & Boundaries 350
Our Pain Becomes Their Power 351
Don't Fear Home 353

Perspectives & Treasures

Buried Treasure 356
Buried Cities 358
Storms 360
Treasures 362
Shape Shifter 364
Celtic Breath 366
When Trees Speak 368
Monumental Gauntlet 370
Twists & Turns 371
Bits of Wisdom 372
Beneath the Leaves 373
A Favorable Wind 374
Mightier 375

Stories, Guides & Whispers of Love

Dishonored But Not Disgraced 378
The Three Masters 380
The Owl and the Treasure 382
Tea Party 384
The Faerie 387
The Dragon's Wings 389
The Goddess and the Bear 391
The Quickening 393
My Raven 395
Dragon's Breath 396
Passion Expressed 400
Wisps 402
About the Author 405

Foreword

Along my ongoing awakening and healing journey, I've learned many ancient healing modalities for emotional and spiritual healing. Messages for shedding skins and shells and rising out of the ashes are shared in the poetic messages in this book. After becoming certified in Reiki and Hypnotherapy, I became certified as a Shamanic practitioner. Over the period of about three years, I wrote eight books of poetic healing messages. This book contains many which tie in with shamanic training and practices for healing on many levels and releasing what no longer serves.

Shamanic Healing work involves and includes journey work, meditative journeys where we meet guides to help us heal any manner of issues. Some of the poetic messages shared here will be like taking short journeys when you read them. Certain ones resonate more deeply with different people. Often they make one go deeply into areas where work is needed, where things need to be acknowledged, thanked, forgiven and released. They offer ideas for working through issues. They offer tools.

Everyone is on their own healing journey. The messages here are to promote deeper thinking; to remind us of the importance of forgiveness for true freedom, to release guilt, shame, resentment, grief, anger, fear, sadness and unforgiveness, in order to clear energetic blocks so energy can flow freely for our well-being on many levels. Each experience and response is unique. This is a reminder of your magnificence and your worthiness and to remember to love yourself.

Janine Palmer (Silver Moon) CHT

Sacred Temple

Darkness and Silence

She went into the silence,
To that holy sacred space,
The domain of love and wisdom,
A primordial comforting place.

By opening herself to the knowledge,
And the wisdom she desired,
Waves of peace and sacred love,
Was the experience which transpired.

Waves of soothing love,
Settled upon her inside an out,
And answers then presented themselves,
To whatever she wondered about.

Beings appeared to her there,
Brightly glowing in colorful rays of light,
Emanating higher degrees of love,
Endless compassion their might.

She experienced forms of healing,
On levels before unknown,
Healing in all her bodies,
She was being shown.

She was shown the need for balance,
In all levels of her being,
Emotional, mental, physical and spiritual,
Raising vibrations so they can sing.

They brought an awareness to the pain she carried,
Unbeknownst to her,
Which blocked her energy from flowing,
And releasing it improved her verve.

Energy began to swirl and flow,
Allowing her light again to move,
Releasing perceptions of judgments,
Pain or anything to prove.

She let go of outdated belief systems,
Which her inner truth knew were lies,
And she could now be her true authentic self,
By shedding her disguise.

Thank you to the silence,
The void, the truth and the kingdom,
For there in the darkness were answers,
Peace and calm and freedom.

Janine Palmer (Silver Moon)

Capstone

That mystical deep connection between souls,
When their hearts sing to one another,
The way they will risk their mortal life,
To save their beloved sister or brother.

These are the qualities of the higher self,
The flickering of the capstone,
Flickering as it does in and out of sight,
Sometimes as flesh and bone.

Our pyramid of light, our temple,
Which is hidden safely within,
At times the capstone seems to be missing,
Then it might appear bearing a grin.

We have to be open to observe it,
We can't see it from ego's level,
That lower level of veils and illusions,
The shadow side also known as the devil.

Even though it might not always be visible,
And somehow not in plain sight,
Our capstone is in our presence and always with us,
Even through the soul's dark night.

Many are not fully aware,
They have everything they need,
It's just on the other side of fear,
Judgment, doubt and greed.

You pyramid is mighty,
A fortress strong and true,
It's the visible and the invisible,
The complex mixture that is you.

Open to the mystery,
Trust your intuitive gifts,
Buckle up baby,
As you flow through this amazing shift.

Janine Palmer (Silver Moon)

Your Temple

What is the temple, the tower of grace?
The facets of you, through time and space,
It's the truth of your soul and the wisdom gained,
To shred the veil and break free of the chains.

There are angels around you, some known and some not,
Here to remind you of things you forgot,
Will you open your heart, your temple door?
To embrace the mysteries you've known before?

Your temple will serve you, the kingdom within,
To rise above nefarious illusions of sin;
You wake when you realize your origin divine,
And that you are a branch of an interconnected vine.

When you nurture your soul with unconditional love,
When you understand and live, as below so above,
The treasure of the kingdom in heaven, in you,
Will reflect divine light in all that you do.

You'll radiate love like a cosmic light,
And share your wisdom so pure and bright,
Honor your temple and honor your Lord,
Your ascension will propel you through unknown doors.

Through those doorways you'll find cosmic gifts,
And you will learn to heal painful rifts,
You will rise above your lower self,
Remembering your divinity, your temple, your wealth.

Janine Palmer (Silver Moon)

Sanctity – The Woods

In the woods she found such sanctity,
It was the woods which nurtured her soul,
The trees spoke to her heart and soul,
And brilliant was their glow.

The trees were keepers of ancient wisdom,
They anchored heaven and earth,
And if one listened to them speak,
There was guidance for rebirth.

Their beauty was indescribable,
What was whispered on the breeze,
Rustling through was spirit,
Creating music through needles and leaves.

A symphony of nature,
A temple in disguise,
Only revealed to those who had awakened,
To see through divinity's eyes.

A mystical dance of the ages,
As they existed in space and time,
In light and shadow and intoxicating fragrance,
Connecting us all to the vine.

Connected as they are to heaven and earth,
By divine branches and divine roots,
And energies at work unseen,
As we reconnect with our truth.

Janine Palmer (Silver Moon)

The Druid Tree

The Druid Tree was ancient,
It was centuries old in this time,
And the wisdom emanating from it,
Was mystical and sublime.

She was a High Priestess of the Order,
She was love in motion and flow,
An earth goddess for the people,
And the tree did nurture her glow.

She found a hidden entrance,
To an inner part of the tree,
And when she entered into it,
She entered a dimension where she was free.

Within the sacred chamber,
Of the Druid Tree divine,
She could hear the songs of angels,
So free of space and time.

And it was there that she was nurtured,
With the pure energy of divine love,
And it was there that she was greeted by,
The raven and the dove.

The animals were so drawn to her,
Because of the love she contained,
Because of the love she freely shared,
Unconditional and unrestrained.

And the love she gave back to the tree,
Made it a beautiful temple indeed,
And through the flow of love above and below,
So much earthly pain was released and freed.

Janine Palmer (Silver Moon)

Monastery

Create a monastery as a healing space,
Somewhere sacred to reflect and heal,
A physical place, a sanctuary,
A place you can touch and feel.

It can be in a building or somewhere in nature,
It can be room, a cave or an empty church,
A place where you can connect with yourself and spirit,
A place for healing, release and rebirth.

The sanctuary can be a safe place you go to,
Even if only in your mind,
A place of your creation,
Where there are answers for you to find.

Take that sacred time for yourself,
Take the time to reflect and to heal,
Release what no longer serves you,
And remember your inner truth no one can steal.

Your inner truth belongs to you,
It's something you do not need to defend,
It's unique to you and yours alone,
Wisdom is always added, learning never ends.

Claim your place as your own,
It is sacred and it is safe,
It is your entrance to higher dimensions,
Your very own garden gate.

Janine Palmer (Silver Moon)

Mysterious Gate

She entered into a cave for healing,
Not knowing what form it would take,
She laid down on a bed of leaves,
And let her mind enter through a mysterious gate.

And who should she meet but an angel,
Who wrapped her warmly in his wings so great,
He sang to her lonely heart and her battered soul,
Releasing old programs, sadness, resentment and hate.

Lifting falsehoods and illusions,
Lifting away guilt and shame and fear,
Lifting away any unforgiveness lingering there,
And washing away any sacred tears.

Lifting her spirit which was part of God,
Healing her heart and soul on higher levels,
To disconnect from the stagnant illusions,
Which create challenging energies we identify as demons and devils.

She remembered coming back through the mysterious gate,
Feeling as if she were floating on a cloud,
Feeling full of the most exquisite love,
Hearing the voice of her own spirit now very clear and loud.

To open to heal all parts of ourselves,
Is something all of us can do,
Just call in your angels and guides for healing,
And open to the blessings which will then come through.

Janine Palmer (Spirit Silver Moon)

Glimpses of Soul

Divine Flame

What is this beauty of her divine flame?
Is there no language which can give it a name?
This breath of fresh air, an angel in our midst;
A twinkling of remembrance, of Divinity's kiss.

Who is this enchanting goddess of light?
Of the Sun by day and the moon by night;
Who are the beings which recognize, here and on other dimensions,
The secret ties remembered, of cherished ancient connections?

Playing out the poetry, of their deep affections;
Mirroring each other boldly, lost in timeless reflection;
To honor the purpose of higher intention;
To answer the call of a higher dimension.

Vibrations which radiate such a brilliant verve,
Their purpose is for love and they come here to serve;
Messengers and healers to their brother man;
A reminder of the presence, of the Divine Light of I AM.

Janine Palmer (Silver Moon)

Our Goddess

She was a goddess for the people,
She was there to heal them with love,
She represented the balance between dark and light,
She reflected the wisdom of the raven and the divinity of the dove.

She appeared one day in a sacred wood,
She wore a crimson velvet dress,
Her hair was a dark as the raven's wing,
And in her presence I was blessed.

She blessed me with the kindest words,
She surrounded me with love so strong,
She lifted my battered spirits,
She sang to me my very own song.

She reflected me back to me,
In a way I couldn't see before,
She reminded me of my importance,
Which then opened bright new doors.

She emanated a delightful energy,
Of love and such brilliant light,
She sat with me for hours,
Sharing the wisdom of second sight.

I am thankful for the gifts which arrive,
To humanity from the Divine,
Sent here to heal us on earth,
To remember our magnificence so fine.

Janine Palmer (Silver Moon)

Echoes of the Soul

My soul whispered to me of soul mates,
Known from times through eternity past,
That our love keeps reuniting us,
Because that love will ever last.

Because we have work to do here,
To remind each other of our worth,
Since we forget it when we descend here,
Until from our own ashes we find rebirth.

When we tear a hole in the veil,
When we break out of our shell,
When life manages to crack us open,
Light shines in and no more hell.

Echoes of my soul's song,
Were faint whispers to me at first,
Then they became louder and more familiar,
And I became reacquainted with my worth.

I discovered I am ever worthy,
Because I am of the Divine,
I'm a co-creator with beloved Source,
And divine light ever intertwines.

Beloved are our soul mates,
So many of them here,
They have reflected me back to me,
And reminded me of love so dear.

We come here because we have work to do,
We must walk this crooked path,
We must find the treasures within us,
We must free ourselves from our masks.

Janine Palmer (Silver Moon)

hold Space

Some people struggle greatly, not showing the love within,
Life has forced them to their knees,
So they surround themselves with armor,
And they carry the burden of grief.

They haven't made the journey out of the ashes,
They haven't forgiven others or themselves,
They exist in their own creation,
Of a debilitating hell.

Can you hold a space for them?
Can you offer your hand in love?
Can you show them there is hope?
On the wings of a healing dove…

Janine Palmer (Silver Moon)

Mists of Spirit

The Wolf spirit was a frequent visitor,
To her dream time in other realms,
Where her soul journeyed other-dimensionally,
When it escaped the illusions which in the physical dwell.

She built a fire beneath the trees,
Their sheltering arms reached to the heavens,
She drew a circle there in the fertile ground,
To see what spirit might choose now to leaven.

Then he appeared there before her,
In her sacred circle upon the ground,
Dancing for her in the swirling mists,
A familiar and healing sound.

He came bearing the gift of the Creators love,
He came with love for her heart,
He came with guidance, wisdom and hope,
A blessing with a message to impart.

He said stand in your truth my beloved,
Wear the mantle of the goddess of the moon,
And what you need for the work on your path,
Will appear to you now very soon.

You come from a place of the greatest love,
You come from compassion's kind flame,
And because of your presence upon this earth,
Many paths for the better you will change.

Janine Palmer (Silver Moon)

The Magic of the Soul

It took many years for me to awaken,
Initiations brought me to my knees,
When they cracked me open for the light to enter,
I began to fathom very deep and mysterious things.

I opened my mind to study the mysteries,
On many levels I began to learn and grow,
My heart and my mind blossomed like flowers,
And from the depths of my soul came a luminous glow.

I began to burn off outdated belief systems,
With a match I sent them alight,
The fire burned away dark falsehoods,
And programmed misconceptions swiftly took flight.

My soul had opened to remember,
Things my higher self already knows,
And my connection to my beloved Creator,
By leaps and bounds now grows.

I'm in gratitude for the darkness,
Which thrust me into the light,
And for the connection I've made with soulmates,
And for my inner light so bright.

I'm thankful for the love I share,
And for the love I continue to receive,
I'm thankful to have risen out of the ashes,
And moved into knowing and out of belief.

Janine Palmer (Silver Moon)

White Thorn

Shamanic healers and goddesses,
Energy here now restored,
For the ascension of the spirit,
Now and from before.

She is an enigma on this planet,
She is a curious piece to a maze,
She is so many things to so many beings,
She is part of the Ancient of Days.

She is a master, a healer and a teacher,
She is a messenger here on Earth,
Some of them could recognize and see her,
Those who were going through a re-birth.

Those in touch with higher levels,
Of the vibration of the collective around,
Of unity consciousness in ascension,
Whose inner truth had finally been found.

But those who still were sleeping,
Couldn't recognize the gifts from Grace,
They who can't see past their judgment and illusion,
To the truth found in anyone's face.

She is in part a Priestess,
Once upon a time, then and now,
She represents hope for so many people,
And it was God who showed her how.

Once upon an ancient time,
White Thorn had been her name,
White for the purity of her soul,
And the thorn for the warrior's game.

Even though it was the strength of compassion,
Which coursed through her spirit and veins,
She was the strength of an army in tiny from,
And she would beat them at their own game.

The Grace of God did fuel her,
Her compassion an elixir so blessed,
She served the collective with love and truth,
And when they hurt her they angels wept.

But her spirit was of a mysterious strength,
And she continued to bless and serve,
Some of them recognized her rare energy,
And they enjoyed her radiant verve.

Those who in ignorance had harmed her,
Learning as they walked along their path,
She forgave them holding space for them in compassion,
Always giving and taking her power back.

She had been known by many names,
During her many missions to this plane,
But he would always remember her as White Thorn,
The Priestess of God's truth which reigned.

Janine Palmer (Silver Moon)

Little Fields

Looking down from a higher perspective,
Little fiends you might see,
Of opportunities for great things,
For endless and exciting possibilities.

For you are a co-creator here,
A creator of good or bad,
At least that is the perception from duality,
And whether you feel happy or sad.

You are a creator of experience,
And what you learn from that,
How you learn to bend and flow,
As you wear many coats and hats.

What field will you nurture?
What field will you tend?
What type of field will draw you?
Because the fields of opportunity never end.

Fields are always created,
For what they will provide,
Whether important lessons or bounty,
They are dependent on one another however they abide.

And with us are silent helpers,
When we endeavor to tune in,
When we find goodness, stillness and happiness,
In between the struggle and the din.

Janine Palmer (Silver Moon)

Mystery & Grace

Dancing Flame

An elegant, wild flame of light,
Danced within her heart,
She began to light her own way,
Out of places gray and dark.

She fanned the flame with intention,
She kindled it with holy breath,
Every time she let go of the old,
She passed another test.

The eyes of her soul were a twinkle,
With the Mystery's cosmic glow,
She danced with the gypsy's light step,
To open each new door.

She sang a song of sweetness,
To her very own beautiful soul,
She was in rhythm with the universe,
And its circular dancing flow.

She whispered on the winds to wise men,
She called to souls not awake,
She shined her light for them with love and compassion,
Upon the Creator's mysterious gate.

Her laugh was a melodious musical strain,
Like the tinkling of many bells,
And the light she shined upon humanity,
Cracked open their darkened shells.

God had sent her to heal the people,
The animals and the trees,
Her love was whispered through hill and dale,
On still days through storms and the breeze.

Those who were meant to hear it,
Would open like so many flowers,
She encouraged them to tap into,
Their very own God-given powers.

She shared her love from a holy place,
The Holy Spirit worked through her,
She was to share the message with humanity,
That for every ailment there was a cure.

She was the nurturing energy of the Divine Feminine,
The Mother to cradle them all,
Her compassionate flame burned brightly for them,
A beloved gift from the All.

Janine Palmer (Silver Moon)

My Light

We might write about things when we feel them,
Even as they unfold,
We begin to speak of these stories,
Even before they are told.

We see a glimmer of light,
Gleaming out from an opening door,
To a feeling of love slightly different,
Than we have ever felt before.

When we open to the mystery,
Expecting nothing in return,
The candle of enlightenment,
Begins to glow and burn.

When we are humble in spirit,
When we listen to our soul,
When we stand in a place of gratitude,
We hear the bell begin to toll.

The bell is calling us to our self,
It's bringing attention to our journey and fate,
Because we wrote it in our soul contracts,
And we recognize the open gate.

We must give ourselves permission,
To experience what we must,
For learning growth and expansion,
From a level of inner trust.

We must come from a place of compassion,
We must treat other people well,
We must not dish out any nastiness,
We wouldn't want to experience our self.

Because karma is about balance,
Life is a balancing act,
It's about learning from experience,
About who's in the looking glass.

Treat others with some dignity,
Treat others with much respect,
Treat them with the kindness you'd like to receive,
And your own honor do not neglect.

As I patiently walked my path alone,
Even with someone else,
A being appeared on my journey,
And caused me to trip a little over myself.

Because I recognized the truest friend,
A love rattling on in and out of time,
Because I am part of his soul,
And because he is part of mine.

I thank the Creative Forces,
For the angels and guides they send,
And I thank myself for opening up,
For learning to flow and bend.

For discovering that truth,
Is something inside myself,
And that the illusion I have been swimming in,
Here on earth is not my hell.

I am grateful to this ancient soul,
Who holds a mirror up for me to see,
And for the love and trust and loyalty,
He continues to show to me.

Janine Palmer (Silver Moon)

The Surface

Just beneath the surface,
Of what you think you see,
Are other deeper layers,
Of what make up you and me.

Layers of beauty and goodness,
Layers of compassion and grace,
And also layers of pain and untold stories,
Which sometimes flicker across our face.

The things which we have buried,
The things we need to release,
The triggers and the healing wisdom,
Interwoven are all of these.

Parts in the process of healing,
Things we cherish and embrace,
Our light and shadow, the balance,
Strength and the doubts and fear we face.

Beneath the surface of everyone,
Are so many things we can't see,
Swirling around affecting us on so many levels,
It's all part of the Mystery.

Because we don't know what affects a person,
Because we don't know all they have been through,
Or how they crumbled or rose above,
It's an unknown variable stew.

Because we don't know what's been processed,
Because we don't know what's been released,
Because we don't know what's in the process of healing,
And we don't know their joy or their grief.

We should hold a space of kindness,
A space of compassion and patience serene,
Because everyone is a teacher to us,
Be open to the wisdom you'll glean.

Janine Palmer (Spirit Silver Moon)

Tresses

In the mists of the forest one morning,
She found a treasure there,
Secrets like words seemed to whisper,
Through the tresses of her raven hair.

The treasure was contained in the secrets,
The mysteries were there to unfold,
They were pieces of her ancient memories,
Like flecks in a stream of gold.

They were pieces of her own wisdom,
Being revealed again to her there,
An awareness of her connection to the collective,
And these were her gifts now to share.

Her hair was a force of energy,
It cascaded down to her waist,
The breeze sent it flying around her,
In a vortex of her mysterious grace.

Her raven appeared there before her,
She held her arm up high,
He alighted gently upon her wrist,
As leaves swirled round in the sky.

He shared with her wisdom he'd gathered,
Revealing things from her lifetimes past,
To show her more clearly a picture,
Of her calling, her mission, her path.

She had already heard the call of her soul,
She accepted her mission for the Divine,
She took up the mystical mantle,
Again here in this space and time.

She had journeyed here many times before,
She was known for her pure heart and soul,
She was loved by the people, their goddess,
And she shared with them her luminous glow.

She opened more fully to the Mystery,
Deeper knowing was revealed to her there,
Which blended back into her light energy,
While light beams danced off her hair.

Her long raven tresses held the secrets,
Of this world and many more,
And with initiates who were now ready,
She would show them Divinity's door.

Janine Palmer (Silver Moon)

Open to the Gifts

As I open up to know myself,
To my purpose and treasures within,
I discover countless valuable things,
New doors open again and again.

It's a mystery and it's intriguing,
To find out more about who I am,
What is my purpose for the greater good?
I learn from experiences whether I fall or stand.

The depth of my strength keeps unfolding,
My compassion knows no bounds,
My heart and my soul guide my journey,
In gratitude blessings are found.

We have the power to heal, others and ourselves,
Forgiveness is a crucial key,
Until we realize there's nothing to forgive,
When we move from 'I' to 'We'.

At higher levels of awareness,
High above duality's snare,
We acknowledge the purpose of experience,
For the wisdom we gain there.

At higher levels above illusions,
Above programming, conditioning and lies,
It's not about ego or right or wrong,
It's about what we do with our lives.

How did our errors direct us?
What did we learn from the pain?
Let go of attachment which causes suffering,
Find your strength and truth once again.

Remember the keys to the kingdom,
They are with you all the time,
You hold the keys and the answers,
In your heart and soul they abide.

Janine Palmer (Silver Moon)

White Wolf

The White Wolf appears to initiates,
The White Wolf in the form of a guide,
Is really an angel in different form,
Appearing to those who no longer hide.

To those who don't hide from the Mystery,
The seekers who study and learn,
The spiritual students on this plane,
Who through transformative fires have burned.

The angel presenting in such a way,
That will resonate on a spiritual level,
So much more than he really seems,
Helping those who rise above devils.

Those who now stand in their power,
They who have entered the kingdom within,
The warriors of the light tribes,
Who recognize the falsehood of sin.

And so they are guided in Divine Love,
And so they have answered the call,
And so they are lifted to higher levels,
As they ascend homeward toward the All.

Janine Palmer (Silver Moon)

Mystical & Sacred

The Eagle and the Raven

Sometimes in other dimensions,
She flies on the wings of the divine,
Sometimes she flies with the eagle,
They fly beyond space and time.

Together they fly for ascension,
In and out of the cosmic dream,
They communicate on levels of higher consciousness,
Because there is more knowledge and wisdom to glean.

Their spirits go wandering in the nether-worlds,
While their physical bodies are fast asleep,
They shift into hidden worlds to share,
Secrets of the Mysteries so deep.

They gather their bits of wisdom,
Their spirits reunite like they are one,
Then they return to their bodies in the lower world,
To shine forth the light of the Sun.

Janine Palmer (Silver Moon)

Walking Between Worlds

We are drawn to the material,
To this physical plane,
It's what we see and feel,
In this life-school game.

But some will also realize,
Their deep connection to spirit,
They feel it and embrace it,
And when it speaks they hear it.

It's a very curious balance here,
The mixture between the two,
Some know how to let it flow,
They allow the mystery to flow through.

Maybe we sense a connection,
To things unseen so deep,
Feelings of love eternal,
Which are ours to keep.

To connect with our inner knowing,
Our intuition is our guide,
Or to ignore that deeper part of ourselves,
And from it we might hide.

We walk between two worlds
Although some of us recognize it not,
Some would rather follow along quite blindly,
With certain things that they were taught.

Others delve into the mystery,
They embrace the secrets of life,
They allow the flow of truth,
To blossom, unfold and ignite.

Do you embrace the Mystery?
Are you content to let some things be unknown?
Do you continue to learn and evolve?
Are you open to new wonders shown?

Or do you shut down in fear?
Do you cling to any programming taught?
Do you think you have all the answers?
Do you feel stuck with the things you bought?

Re-connecting with divinity,
Might mean detaching from this physical world,
In prayer and meditation,
And in openness blessings unfurl.

To embrace the mystical side of you,
The ethereal part of this life,
When we disengage from our ideas about things,
We then rise up out of strife.

When we whisper love without our words,
When we share with others the love that we are,
That is when we find balance here,
And that's how we heal the wounds underneath the scars.

Janine Palmer (Silver Moon)

Experiences

Layers and layers of experience,
Are wrapped around who we are,
We flicker in and out of the mystery,
Trying to remember who we are.

Part of us knows unexplainable things,
Part of us lingers in the dark,
Part of us is ever tapped into the light,
Guided as we are by our spark.

Some of us know of the spark of God,
Which is hidden in the safest place,
Our kingdom within, our sacred heart,
The glorious smile of Divinity's face.

Janine Palmer (Silver Moon)

Forces

What is this fire which you often breathe?
Is a negative reaction what you hope to receive?
Do dragons fly through summer skies?
Could you recognize an imposter in disguise?

Beware of the invaders who may try to interfere,
And the negativity which threatens that which we hold dear,
Positive forces which keep the fire from your breath,
The very same protection which keeps our love from death.

When moonlight bathes the valley in an iridescent glow,
Remember that my love for you is all you need to know,
My heart is a castle, my love is strong and deep,
You are my knight protector, defender of my keep.

When dusk settles lowly across the land,
Remember the moonlight and take my hand,
There is light to be shared in you and I,
Doves fly through the summer sky.

Janine Palmer (Silver Moon)

The Tree at Twilight

He took her there one evening,
Holding her hand as he guided her in,
To an enchanted place hidden in the trees,
Where the veil between dimensions was thin.

The tree stood beside a still pond,
And twilight shone through its branches extended,
But in the reflection of the tree in the pond,
Were light rays glowing as they swirled and blended.

Reflecting the light beams so mystically,
Reflections of another dimension,
And to connect with that reality,
Was to create by one's intentions.

And music began to filter through,
From angels and faeries in their midst,
And a breeze wafted in to caress her cheek,
Or was it an angel's bold kiss?

The experience there did touch her soul,
On a level she could not quite explain,
But she would be healed and called by the divine,
And she would never again be the same.

Janine Palmer (Silver Moon)

The Raven's Call

In the shadows he stood in wisdom,
Silhouetted by golden light,
He held the keys to the Mysteries,
Of the battles of wrong and right.

That on higher dimensional levels,
It's not about right or wrong,
When we rise above duality and illusion,
We hear the Oneness song.

But the lower levels test us,
Our mettle and our might,
To rise above and ascend back home,
Because there is no longer any reason to fight.

The raven's call did reach her,
In ways she didn't yet understand,
But also calling to her was the voice of the dove,
And their combined power was in her hands.

Janine Palmer (Silver Moon)

On her Journey

On a shamanic journey,
Where her soul experienced other dimensions,
She would do important healing work there,
Based off of pure love and higher intention.

Amazing planes were visited,
And the guides who would appear,
In many forms so familiar,
Who helped her energy to clear.

And the knowledge gained was priceless,
Forgotten wisdom was being regained,
And in reconnecting with her higher self,
She was released from many chains.

Disconnection from so many illusions,
Open to other perceptions which would appear,
New perspectives to open new doors,
And the infinite love of the Divine conquering fears.

A warrior goddess of the Light,
And her journeys to different worlds,
Was part of creative experience itself,
As it changed and blossomed and unfurled.

And then the drum beat changed,
And the reality of now was calling her back,
And she could only smile in amazement,
At the new treasures she now carried in her sack.

The medicine bag and the mesa,
Sacred items for Sacred Medicine Space,
Just a few pieces of the Shaman's tools,
Interwoven with the Creator's infinite Grace.

Janine Palmer (Silver Moon)

Divine Wisdom & Energy

Medicine Speaks

Don't let it have power over you,
Don't let your courage turn to fear,
Your mission here is greater than you know,
The dysfunction is why you are here.

Open your heart to let in pure love,
Open your soul's eye to see,
Open your mind in wonder,
Don't let it be closed in belief.

Honor your brother as yourself,
Honor all animals divine,
Don't think you're superior in any way,
It's not about yours or mine.

Speak with a whisper from your heart,
You speak without words to the divine,
Be open to discover your gifts,
You've carried with you throughout time.

Janine Palmer (Silver Moon)

Turn the Page

Whether it's a lesson,
Or whether it's a gift,
Take the love and understand,
What you've gained and make a shift.

Don't remain too long in energy,
Which definitely doesn't serve you,
Or the forward movement on your journey,
What have you learned from what you went through?

Don't allow yourself to remain stuck,
In the lower energies of that pain
Swim your way to the surface,
To the light there to be gained.

Energy needs to move,
It always needs to flow,
And if you continue to move with it,
Blessings will be bestowed.

Giving thanks for knowledge gained,
Release what holds you back,
Regain the power of your divinity,
Do not identify with lack.

Because whatever you choose to focus on,
You will receive more of the same,
Thoughts are powerful, thoughts create,
You are in control of your own game.

Don't give away your power,
To thoughts which are not true,
Tap into the powerful force,
And the love that is in you.

Janine Palmer (Silver Moon)

Branches of Moonlight

She ventured nightly into the woods,
To feel the healing energy there,
The tranquil peace she felt from the trees,
And the energy they freely shared.

She would ask them curious questions,
Without speaking any words,
And the answers coming through her higher self,
Told her she was heard.

Where do I really come from?
And what am I connected to?
What is this force which drives me?
And how does it come through?

What are these ancient truths,
Which tumble from my lips?
And why when the sun goes down,
Does moonlight glow from my fingertips?

I am grounded to the earth by roots,
Which are interconnected with the trees,
They whisper to me ancient wisdom,
And they are always eager to please.

They told me the beauty of silver moonlight,
Emanates through my being,
And sometimes I might be blinded by light,
Which my physical eyes aren't seeing.

What pathways have I walked?
And how did they help me grow?
What experiences throughout time,
Have forged the substance of my soul?

As I walk this crooked path,
Dodging life's traps and clever snares,
I find a deeper connection to my higher self,
Letting go of earthy cares.

I add to my bag of wisdom,
And I add to my bag of tools,
I mustn't judge things I can't understand,
Even from apparent fools.

I have learned so much about healing,
About forgiving and letting go,
The more things that I learn,
The more I realize I don't know.

I ride a river of energy,
Fed by magnificent Source,
And the power which is all around us,
Is love the most powerful force.

There is so much more to creation,
Than we can touch or see or feel,
And it is our heart and soul,
Which lets us know it's real.

The perspective of our Creator,
Means different things to different people,
We can worship in manmade structures or in nature,
But we are the sacred steeples.

A light shines from us to our Creator,
And our Creator shines light back,
When we see past the webs of illusion,
We will discover there is nothing we lack.

I am the love of many,
Of so many lessons which flow from my heart and soul,
I feel compassion for many beings,
And they recognize love's glow.

I am a divine messenger and a heretic,
I AM God's warrior walking out of the dark,
The more I connect with my higher self,
The brighter glows my spark.

As I continue to do my self-work,
It brings more clarity to the things I see,
And the more I accept the differences of others,
Then the more do I accept me.

These are things the trees taught me,
As their branches anchor in heaven,
And through my initiations,
I've learned more about God, the One, the Three, the Seven.

The seven creative beings who are the Elohim,
Spoken about in Genesis and to us there they're shown,
They who created man in their image,
Spirit combined with matter, which made the physical known.

So many blessings are bestowed upon us,
In spirit which we cannot see,
Angels and guides who love and care,
Whom we can call on in times of need.

The moonlight is so soothing,
It is a gentle healing force,
The light of the moon's healing energy,
Branches out from me of course.

It speaks to the ocean's tides,
And its primal pull we feel,
And when I share my love from the divine,
I help myself and others to heal.

We need healing from life's trauma's,
From its challenges and initiations,
We must learn to let go of old pain and old patterns,
Because of manifestation.

Your reality will reflect,
The thoughts which you continue to think,
So take charge of that arena,
It's up to you if you swim or sink.

We all need healing on many levels,
Hold nothing against yourself,
Find balance between the bodies,
Emotional, mental, spiritual and physical.

Be aware of the presence of new doors,
And cast off your armor and walls,
Listen to the sweet whisper of your soul,
In silence you will hear the call.

You are a magnificent creator,
In many ways you simply forgot,
That with proper thought and intention,
You will have or you will have not.

Release from your beautiful temple,
Any toxic thing,
Invite in healing on whatever level,
And let your soul hear you sing.

Janine Palmer (Silver Moon)

Teacher

The teacher spoke in a quiet tone,
He said, I want you imagine this,
Picture it in your mind and hold it in your heart,
About what was, what will be, and what is.

He said, Imagine the love of all mothers,
Through space time in eternity,
Through centuries, millennia and the ages,
Can you even imagine what it would be?

Can you imagine the force of that power?
Can you imagine the light glowing from that love?
Can you hear it on the whispers,
Of the wings of the Holy Dove?

He said, Imagine the love of all fathers,
Through space time in eternity,
Through centuries, millennia and the ages,
Can you imagine what it would be?

Can you image the strength of that power?
Can you imagine that strong, protective, fierce love?
Can you feel it from the light of the sun,
Shining down on you from above?

Do you feel it when you're in nature,
Gazing up at the beauty of a tree?
Do you hear it in a babbling brook,
Or in a storm blowing in on a breeze?

Do you feel it in your neighbor,
Or in your brother man,
Do you feel it when you worship God?
Or know it's in a grain of sand.

That love filling the oceans and the land,
That love indefinite through all space,
That love exists in your Sacred Heart,
An eternal state of grace.

Visualize all of that love,
Which the human mind can't comprehend,
And with gratitude send that love to the world,
Because that love is love without end.

Janine Palmer (Silver Moon)

Their healing

If I've learned anything on my journey,
And was asked to share knowledge gained,
It is that no matter how much we might try,
We can't heal everyone else's dark pain.

We can assist them though, if they ask us.
With unconditional love and by sharing wisdom,
But only if they ask in earnest and participate,
This is their journey and their mission.

They have to be fully present,
They have to be active in the endeavor,
They have to let go of attachment and suffering,
They have to flip the switch now or the lever.

Offer an ear to listen,
Offer a hand to hold,
Offer a shoulder to cry on,
But don't take on anyone's load.

Encourage them to let go,
Encourage them to release,
Anything which no longer serves them,
Take the wisdom and decide to be free.

Janine Palmer (Silver Moon)

Living Prayer

A call to prayer, our daily return,
To our Source, the Love for which we burn,
Our prayers we sing for our daily needs,
Spoken or unspoken reflected by our deeds.

When we dry a tear or lend a hand,
When we till the soil and work the land,
When we acknowledge the beauty of nature divine,
These are our prayers, yours and mine.

Do you know you create the life you face?
So our prayer must come from a place of grace,
Because your life is a living prayer,
Be ever mindful of the energy you share.

Ask for healing when you need it, offer it when you can,
To your beloved sister and your beloved brother man,
Remember we are all connected to Source, the Divine, the One,
Our prayer a direct reflection of how we dance under the glorious Sun.

Our prayer is how we share our light,
We tap into knowing what is wrong or right,
This doesn't come from dogma or how man misinterprets facts,
Everything is within us, there is nothing that we lack.

Remember prayer is a living thing,
What will you contribute, what will you bring?
How do you dance and how do you sing?
What reverence do you hold for any holy thing?

Sing from your heart your sacred prayer,
Share with your brother the love you find there,
Honor your divinity, remember your grace,
Be a living prayer, honor sacred space.

Love yourselves O holy ones, as your Creator so loves you,
Remember to recognize the sacred, in everything you do,
You are the light of the world, you are a living prayer,
An endless supply of love in your heart, will ever await you there.

Janine Palmer (Silver Moon)

Wisdom Keepers

Druids, Magi, Shaman,
Or Brahman will it be?
They were all of a similar understanding
Of the mysteries to help man see.

When and where did fear arise,
To take control of man?
With the rulers of the earth,
And then when ego took a stand.

Ego is a servant,
But it should never be in charge,
That's when fear can creep in,
And run randomly at large.

Some tests here are easy,
And some tests here are not,
Some tests are simply about remembering,
Things which we forgot.

Ancient initiates guided the people in understanding,
The existence between mankind and the gods,
Priests and hierophants such as Melchizedek, Moses, Solomon and
    Elijah,
Were divine wisdom keepers of truth which would not be forgotten.

Philosophers taught deeper understandings,
As well as the Druids, Celts and Sages,
Ancient Mysteries were passed to those who were ready,
To receive higher wisdom through continuing, ongoing ages.

Sacred knowledge encompasses astrology,
Astronomy, physics and healing,
Religions, magic, mathematics and architecture,
Sacred geometry and engineering.

The rituals, beliefs and practices of the Druids,
Were very similar to the Hebrew prophets,
But mankind has lost understanding of this,
Due to fear, greed and lust for profit

The Druids followed Melchizedek,
As those in the Bible do,
But the general knowledge of this,
Has largely been lost to me and you.

Janine Palmer (Silver Moon)

What We Learn

What we learn is an overlay,
The knowledge overlays the so-called sin,
The wisdom overlays what we think was wrong,
From any experience where we grow or begin again.

The knowledge and wisdom we extract,
From any person, place or thing,
Is what we learn from the good or the bad,
When we hear the angels sing.

When we understand more deeply,
What anything was trying to teach,
And carry it for healing and forward movement,
It overrides what anyone might preach.

What we do with those pearls of wisdom,
From things we think we did wrong,
From things we think others did wrong to us,
Helps us create new lyrics to our song.

What lessons and wisdom we gained here,
Are more important than the supposed sin we fear,
It might be the very thing which cracks us open,
To our own truth which we begin to hear.

So please don't be too preoccupied,
With particular ideas of sin and hell fire,
Create the reality which reflects your soul,
Because you'll experience what you create by higher or lower desire.

Janine Palmer (Silver Moon)

Your Keys of Sacred Light

To many doors of enlightenment,
It is you who holds the keys,
Within you shines a sacred lamp,
And there is guidance to all of these.

The guides you have may take many forms,
And most will recognize them not,
Many of them might initially be rejected,
Due to the things which you were taught.

This tapestry is your creation,
What will you create with your hands?
How will you rise when life knocks you down?
And for whom will you take a stand?

How swiftly will you listen,
To whispers barely heard?
And when will you discover,
You are the creation of the Word?

How will life's fires transform you?
What will you plant in the ash?
How will you heal yourself now,
From the wounds of earthly lash?

How will you lift a brother,
Or a sister who needs your hand?
How will you honor your ancestors,
In grace upon this sacred land?

Smiles and tears will come and go,
But love will always remain,
Knowing this realm is only temporary,
For the wisdom you will attain.

Eventually you will rise from this illusion,
To hidden truth which will transpire,
As initiations draw upon your warrior's strength,
While you wear this human attire.

And eventually you will shed it,
Because at some point you will need it not,
But the veil of deep illusion and amnesia,
Make your truth a thing you forgot.

No matter what obstacles and battles,
Life seems to throw your way,
The keys to your truth and inner light,
Are with you every day.

When you set down your burdens,
And when you cease in anger to fight,
It is then you will notice a glimmer,
Deep within you, your sacred light.

Janine Palmer (Silver Moon)

Tempo

The tempo of Creation,
The heartbeat of fire and life,
Somewhere between the perception,
Of ongoing blissfulness and strife.

The sounds which are heard or unheard,
On so many levels rippling out,
And the cry of so many beings,
Whether they whisper or they shout.

A matrix all around, a web of connectedness,
The breath of life here which creates,
As we rise above as beings of light,
When we step away from hate.

The drum beat of any heart,
More familiar when known through great love,
With the raven perched on one shoulder,
And on the other shoulder, the dove.

One whispers of the wisdom of the ages,
The other whispers of compassion and truth of the spirit,
But they can only be heard by those quiet enough,
And still enough to hear it.

Even amidst the chaos,
We can find a place of peace,
And when we quiet the monkey mind,
The incessant chatter will begin to cease.

Take yourself on a journey,
Out of this hellish plane,
To reacquaint yourself with the beauty,
Which you came from and need to regain.

Janine Palmer (Silver Moon)

Transformative Fire

Trial by Fire

What challenges do you face,
Which bring you to your knees?
What are they meant to teach you?
What lessons do you glean?

You are in this realm for experiences,
Not about wrong or right;
You must learn to detach from the pain of your thoughts,
Disengage from darkness and embrace sacred light.

What programs are you running?
What thought loops do you constantly replay?
When will you be ready to release them?
And welcome the light of a new day?

You hold the power within you,
The holy power to heal,
It's a gift from your Creator,
That nothing and no one can steal.

Send yourself unconditional love,
From the Highest Source,
To nurture your beautiful soul,
For strength upon your course.

Janine Palmer (Silver Moon)

Resurrected

We are resurrected in the light,
When we take our power back from the dark,
When we hear the eternal call of our soul,
When we feel the light of our own God spark.

On the wings of love are miracles,
In the way of people, places and things,
Even the love from the animals,
Which causes our soul to sing.

Our hearts are filled with God's own light,
Our souls are connected to the All,
God is ever extending a hand to us,
Even when we stumble and fall.

Resurrection is the long-suffering initiation, the act of rising above,
Resurrection is the ascension of our divinely inspired goals,
Resurrection is the true life beyond the physical,
Returning home to the light of the soul.

The flame is the key to our compassion,
The eternal sacred flame,
And once it is ignited in our heart,
We will never be the same.

Janine Palmer (Silver Moon)

The Ashes

I wonder can you see the magic,
Or destruction by what you create,
I wonder do you see closed doors and walls,
Or do you see open windows and garden gates?

Do you see it as a struggle,
Or do you see it as a test?
Do you give without expectation,
Only to find your treasure chest?

Do you expect things from others,
Then feel disappointed when they don't do what you thought?
When what you hoped with no communication,
Transformed into what you wanted not.

Did you take into account other's free will choice?
Do you realize things happen for us to learn?
And that sometimes we must accept and surrender,
And certain thoughts and ideas we must burn.

We must burn away the old,
To clear a space for the new,
We must be a reflection of the honor and Grace,
We would like to see come through.

We must acquaint ourselves with forgiveness,
We must look forward to the opening of new doors,
And not cast our gaze in disappointment,
To the ashes on the floor.

The ashes are the battlegrounds of rebirth,
In the ashes are the remnants of things learned,
The wisdom is what we take with us,
The old pain is what we burn.

The things which appear to be negative,
Serve a purpose if we will but see,
But they are not meant to be carried around with us,
Do you want to be a prisoner or do you want to be free?

Janine Palmer (Silver Moon)

Dragon's Fire

The Dragon was there for a purpose,
Although his presence was at first unknown,
Because she had veered off course on her journey,
And she had an important calling unknown.

She has been too focused on material things,
Which is not what this life is about,
And she had ancient gifts yet undiscovered,
So the Dragon was to help her find out.

The Dragon's fire burned her house down,
Because in the ashes she would find,
A trail to the road of her calling,
To help awaken the spiritually blind.

She would lose the connection with her partner,
She would lose her very best friend,
She would plant seeds in the ashes,
While on a journey for her heart to mend.

She would have to open to healing,
And in the process she would learn how,
And beings of love through soul contracts,
Would appear to show her now.

So she studied and studied and studied,
And she continued to grow and learn,
She learned of the lies of world religions,
And that our magnificence is nothing we earn.

Our magnificence is our essence,
Which organizations would have us disbelieve,
But she learned so many tools for healing,
For rebirth and ascension to achieve.

She had to awaken herself to healing,
She had to learn to detach from her pain,
She was to share what she learned with the beings,
Who appeared on her path unrestrained.

She learned the importance of releasing,
So many things which just don't serve,
Like guilt and shame and fear and judgment,
Which so block our radiant verve.

And so she reconnected with her divinity,
She began to remember her calling divine,
People began to reflect back to her,
A goddess from another place and time.

She began to discover who she was,
She began to realize who she had been,
She began to blossom and open up to,
The phoenix rising out of her ashes again.

She loved the light of awakening,
She loved the color of truth so divine,
She loved the love she gave and received,
And the collective connectedness to the vine.

And the Dragon was always with her,
And the Dragon now did smile,
She was so glad she had become aware of him,
Because the Dragon was a warrior all the while.

The Dragon was a guide protector,
The Dragon knew the depth of her soul,
The Dragon was a strength rare on Earth,
The Dragon helped fuel her glow.

Janine Palmer (Silver Moon)

Frozen Heart, Blade of Fire

She'd volunteered to descend here from higher realms,
To share her light with the Earth,
But to come here she had to go through a veil of forgetting,
Forgetting her value and worth.

She would do her good works by her intuition,
Even though her home she'd forgotten,
She was still able to shine an incredible light,
To those who were stumbling and downtrodden.

A day arrived when she felt earth life was too harsh,
Due to cruelty, fear, greed and lies,
She laid down upon a frozen lake with her sword upon her chest,
Feeling like her inner flame had died.

She surrendered her spirit to a higher power,
And she said, 'I know I don't belong here,'
Her glorious spirit lifted out of her body,
And she found herself in her home so dear.

Total recall was restored to her of her identity,
She was a master on a sacred mission to help,
From the collective higher dimensional angelic planes,
She had descended here into this hell.

It wasn't really hell but it felt that way,
So much lower than the higher conscious realm she knew,
She came from a higher consciousness of unconditional love,
And had descended into duality to help the few.

She was to help the few who would listen,
And to open to their goodness within,
That they might open to the truth of illusion,
And to the trap of believing in sin.

On earth one is so disconnected,
From higher consciousness and trapped in lies,
Trapped in the illusions of fear and forgetfulness,
Hiding behind masks and disguise.

She was one of many here to assist,
In liberating humanity on the wings of the dove,
She was one of many courageous warriors,
Making a sacrifice from unconditional love.

To awaken as many as possible,
To the unity of Oneness and abundant fullness all around,
To wake up to and be aware to the trappings of duality,
To higher blessings which ever abound.

The knight saw a glimmer in the frozen lake,
Glinting for a moment in the sun,
He drew nearer to check it, a curious thing,
His adventure had only begun.

He stepped onto the lake and to his surprise,
A woman lay just under the surface,
The intermittent sunlight reflected off her sword,
Why was she there, what was the purpose?

Then he knelt there above her
And for her he began to pray,
He prayed for the soul of this beauty,
In her watery grave where she lay.

Her spirit above in higher realms,
Could see him kneeling there,
Her heart was warmed by the energy he shared,
And the kind-hearted way he showed he cared.

He prayed from a place of unconditional love,
Which was a miraculous healing power,
And that love permeated interstellar dimensions,
Causing light waves to dance and to flower.

She decided it was time to come back,
For her spirit to enter her frozen shell,
His prayers created magic there,
Causing her sword to glow and the ice to melt.

He stood and walked off the ice,
And then he couldn't believe his eyes,
The sword which lay on top of her glowed bright orange,
Melting the encasement of ice.

The ice crackled all around,
And there was a swirling of frozen mists,
Never had this courageous knight,
Seen anything such as this.

To his further amazement,
The fair lady then opened her eyes,
His chin nearly fell to the ground,
Such was the surprise.

Somehow in a foggy ice-filled mist,
She raised herself out of the lake,
And she glided over to thank him for his prayers,
To thank him for true love's sake.

He wrapped his cloak around her,
And asked if she was okay,
She told him she was fine,
And that it was a very special day.

She told him of the power,
Of his unconditional prayer,
And because of the love he'd sent to her soul,
She was no longer laying there.

Janine Palmer (Silver Moon)

The Stake

Let's talk about the representation,
Let's talk about the stake,
Let's talk about those who sleep,
And let's talk about those who are awake.

Let us first acknowledge,
Most who sleep are aware of it not,
They believe the illusion of the dream they're in,
Their divine truth is temporarily forgotten.

We've all heard the gruesome stories,
Of those who were burned at the stake,
Because of man's obscene greed and ignorance,
And so many spirits they attempted to rape.

To tie any human being to a stake,
And then to set it alight to the fire,
Is the devil incarnate here on the earth,
And through religions, hell doth transpire.

But what the ignorant fools didn't quite understand,
And what they were too blind to see,
Is that when they subjected a being to the fire,
They really just set them free.

Whether it is a stake in the tinder,
Or whether it is a Roman cross,
The fire and brimstone burn away,
The ill effects of the ignorance of lies and dross.

The fire burns away the veil,
The fire is what purifies,
The fire is what transforms,
And burns away the lies.

The perverted sleeping fools in masks,
Masquerading as God's servants here,
Were pawns of darkness existing in hell,
And were guided and directed by fear.

So disconnected from their inner truth,
So disconnected from their kingdom within,
That they believed the lies of illusion from fear,
And their erroneous misinterpretation of sin.

Misinterpretation of sin is ongoing,
To this day it is all around,
To sin means simply to miss the mark,
But that's not what you hear around town.

That's not what the preachers preach from the pulpit,
When it is their intention to instill guilt and fear,
And that my brethren is the biggest sin,
To cause any brother or sister a tear.

But the tears and pain are how we learn,
The mistakes are what re-direct,
For us to find our inner truth,
Do we embrace it or do we reject?

Do we buy into someone's interpretation?
Of the fire and brimstone and lies?
Or do we learn to recognize the imposter,
Do we learn to see past the masks and disguise?

Because when those innocent beings,
Were so callously tied to the stake,
It was to themselves the perpetrators were doing harm,
As they lingered on this side of hell's dark gate.

Those who healed with energy and herbs,
Ancient tools even used by Jesus here,
Were called witches and condemned to death,
All because of ignorance, foolishness and fear.

And those who practiced a truer faith,
Than the one which ruled at the time,
Were persecuted and set to the flame,
These were your brothers and sisters and mine.

But here is what they did not know,
Because what we think we see is not always what is going on,
Because their guardian angels lovingly took their souls beforehand,
And they ascended together from this hell and moved on.

What we might think we see,
Through our limited perception and human eyes,
Is not what is happening on other levels,
We believe the illusions, falsehoods and lies.

So don't be so convinced,
That something you see is wrong,
Because on levels unbeknownst to you,
They are singing a very different song.

Janine Palmer (Silver Moon)

Seek Among the Ashes

She found herself among the ashes,
The kingdom she knew had burned down,
Things looked so much differently now,
But in the ashes were things to be found.

The things which she had trusted,
The things which before were known,
Had burned in transformative fire,
New seeds would now be sown.

And things do grow when ash is tilled,
Into the fertile soil,
Like things which come from hard work and intention,
Form blood and sweat and toil.

But in between the labor,
And in between the gain,
Are periods of rest and reflection,
Along with frustration, doubt and disdain.

Some of it we rise above,
Some of it we sift through,
Some of it will die away,
And new wisdom will come through to you.

The sprouting of ideas,
The things which we create,
Through the dark, the light and the shadow,
Which illuminate doors and gates.

The phoenix will then rise up,
When the time is right for you,
Rebirth will unfold and blossom,
So new blessings can come through.

But we must leave things in the ashes,
Which serve us here no more,
To lighten our weary burdens,
As we walk through those new doors.

Janine Palmer (Silver Moon)

Forms of Healing
& Forgiveness

Nature's Breath

She had been hurled through dark tunnels,
And slammed into closed doors,
She'd experienced being victim,
And victor through many spiritual wars.

She had been forced to her knees,
Where she found great treasure,
She'd come face to face with her soul,
And wisdom she could not measure.

With acceptance of experiences,
And detachment from her pain,
She'd somehow become reacquainted,
With her heart again.

She went into the woods,
And called upon nature to heal,
She found truth within her Self,
Which no one could ever steal.

In the woods she sat and listened,
To the whispers through the trees,
And the ancient knowledge floating on spirit,
Through each and every breeze.

She listened to the animals,
Who spoke softly without words,
And every bit of guidance,
By her heart and soul was heard.

The water told her stories,
Each babbling little stream,
The medicine she found there,
The most healing to be gleaned.

The stunning beauty of Gaia,
So soothing to the senses,
Free and wild and unspoiled,
Caused her to be pensive.

She sat on a bed of pine needles,
Beside a fallen tree,
She breathed in nature's fragrance,
Then closed her eyes to see.

She saw rays of light so brilliant,
Bathing all around,
She heard the music of the universe,
It was the only sound.

She breathed into her heart space,
And let it fill with love,
She felt a presence with her now,
Descended from above.

She felt his wings around her,
Such comfort and such peace,
And she released her burdens to him,
Surrendered, a sacred healing release.

Janine Palmer (Silver Moon)

Open to the Gifts

As I open up to know myself,
To my purpose and treasures within,
I discover countless valuable things,
New doors open again and again.

It's a mystery and it's intriguing,
To find out more about who I am,
What is my purpose for the greater good?
I learn from experiences whether I fall or stand.

The depth of my strength keeps unfolding,
My compassion knows no bounds,
My heart and my soul guide my journey,
In gratitude blessings are found.

We have the power to heal, others and ourselves,
Forgiveness is a crucial key,
Until we realize there's nothing to forgive,
When we move from 'I' to 'We'.

At higher levels of awareness,
High above duality's snare,
We acknowledge the purpose of experience,
For the wisdom we gain there.

At higher levels above illusions,
Above programming, conditioning and lies,
It's not about ego or right or wrong,
It's about what we do with our lives.

How did our errors direct us?
What did we learn from the pain?
Let go of attachment which causes suffering,
Find your strength and truth once again.

Remember the keys to the kingdom,
They are with you all the time,
You hold the keys and the answers,
In your heart and soul they abide.

Janine Palmer (Silver Moon)

Snares

What snares are these in mind and heart,
The soul cries, do beware,
These walls of illusions which block our path,
You won't find your treasure there.

Invite the pain you hold to leave,
Pull it from the temple of your Self,
Thank is for the lessons learned,
Clean that clutter from those shelves.

Breathe in a new and cleansing breath,
Breathe out the old and worn,
Invite the healing angels' light,
Seeing through the veil which has been torn.

The light in you which yearns to shine,
Is from the kingdom of love within,
When you let go of pain and strife,
You let go of sin.

Janine Palmer (Silver Moon)

Well of Forgiveness

Let's heal the pain you carry,
Are you ready to let it go?
Let's release your burdens to your angels on high,
And allow your energy to flow.

Don't hold anything against yourself,
Don't carry guilt, it's a trap,
Don't carry shame, resentment of anger,
Look into your heart and you'll find there's nothing that you lack.

Tap into your well of forgiveness,
And direct it toward yourself,
Then direct it toward anyone else,
To dissolve your self-made prison, where you'll no longer dwell.

Reintroduce yourself to the divine love,
Which is tucked away in your heart,
Where you will come to know yourself again,
And never again will you part.

Janine Palmer (Silver Moon)

Your Cure

Your cure is the love you hold in your heart,
Your cure is your open mind,
Your cure is learning to rise above,
Your cure is detaching from what keeps you blind.

Your cure is forgiveness of yourself,
Your cure is forgiveness of your brother,
Your cure is being in gratitude,
Your cure is holding space for others.

Your cure includes acceptance,
Your cure includes surrender,
Your cure includes releasing old pain,
Your cure is your magnificence to remember.

Your cure is connected to your higher self,
Your cure is rising above ego,
Your cure is in loving yourself,
Your cure is your heart and soul.

Janine Palmer (Silver Moon)

The Flower and her Power

She stood at the edge of a clear stream,
In a tattered calico dress,
Plucking the petals off of a daisy,
Was it from boredom or was it from stress?

She was dropping the petals one by one,
Into the current of the stream,
In a quiet type of meditation,
Rather like a standing dream.

The wind caught her golden-red hair,
Which billowed about her face,
Tendrils of fire lifted in chaos,
But she was the picture of standing Grace.

What was she thinking as she stood there?
What thoughts flitting round in her head?
Was it so much strife and hardship?
Was it sadness from the loss of the dead?

She was releasing any sadness or anger,
Any pain and unforgiveness too,
Every time she plucked a petal and tossed it into the stream,
That was what she would do.

Each little care or worry,
Each little piece of old pain,
She would thank it for what it taught her,
And release the rest for the peace she would gain.

By releasing the demons from her being,
She kept balance and peace for herself,
So she could continue to be present and helpful,
When needed for someone else.

This little remedy so enabled her,
To keep herself in balance and in flow,
Her grandmother had told her long ago,
Any old baggage should not be in tow.

She offered up a prayer of gratitude,
She had made an agreement with the flower,
The flower helped her release her worries,
In order to stand in her power.

Janine Palmer (Silver Moon)

Clean Slate

When we begin to forgive,
To let go or rise above,
We are tapping into a super power,
The super power of love.

When we do the work to clear,
We then prepare a clean slate,
We reintegrate love into our lives,
When we disengage from hate.

When we let go of the illusions which cloud things,
When we release all our burdens to the light,
When we call in our angels for healing,
We rise above our ideas of wrong and right.

We need to be aware of programs,
There are programs we run which hold us back,
Programs like anger, shame, guilt and fear,
Those negative thought loops which keep us in lack.

Be proactive and take responsibility,
For your energy and how you function and feel,
Remember that fear is an illusion,
And love most powerful is always real.

Sit with the uncomfortable thoughts and memories,
And determine what wisdom you gained,
Release the pain which no longer serves you,
Embrace universal and self-love unrestrained.

When you release the burdens,
Created from fears and falsehoods and lies,
Created from misunderstandings and ego,
From that clean slate your butterfly flies.

Tap into your own healing energy,
It is such a powerful force,
Focus on the reality you create here,
You are the navigator of your course.

Janine Palmer (Silver Moon)

Go Into it

She found him sitting at the edge of the wood,
Seeming lost and so deep in thought,
He barely acknowledged her presence when she arrived,
In deep memories he had been caught.

He said, 'I'm working on processing buried emotion,
I'm working on letting things go,
But I get stuck in certain areas,
And how to move past it do not know.'

She said, 'What are working through specifically?
What do you want to release?
What issues have been plaguing you?
I can help you if you tell me please.'

He said, 'I have trouble moving forward,
I have trouble opening myself,
I am not comfortable communicating vulnerability,
It takes me back into that hell.'

She said, 'Go deeper into that feeling,
If you go further into the indecision,
What do you find when you go there?
Parts of you buried or parts of you risen?'

He said, 'I find parts of me buried there,
And I'm afraid to let them out,
I'm afraid the pain will be overwhelming,
And I might cry or scream and shout.'

She said, 'It's okay to allow it to come out,
Every time your mind takes you there,
It's because it wants to be released, my friend,
It wants you to lay it all bare.'

He said, 'When I go to that place of sadness,
I see something I didn't want to face,
I see it buried there for safe keeping,
But it clouds my state of grace.'

She said, 'And what if you opened the door to it,
Open it a crack just to see,
If it's something you can face now,
If you're ready to set it free."

He agreed and he said he opened the door,
And it wasn't as bad as it seemed,
He gathered his courage opening the door all the way,
And let out the old pain which once had silently screamed.

He released it now to the light,
No longer his burden to carry anymore,
And he felt lighter and freer and happier now,
That he'd opened another door.

He looked at her and he smiled,
And he gathered her in his arms,
'Thank my dear friend for your presence,
And for your radiant healing charm.'

Janine Palmer (Silver Moon)

Smoke

I wrote my thoughts down on a page,
Of things I was ready to let go,
I released those feelings from myself,
To clear my light to glow.

I am ready to heal from old pain,
To process the emotions I had buried,
To eject the heavy useless burdens,
I realized I should no longer carry.

I wrote down what I learned,
From experiences and events,
From people and situations,
And things started to make sense.

I see clearly that I was redirected,
Along this path of life,
And I must detach from my ideas about it,
To disconnect from the prison of strife.

I took that page of my thoughts,
Of pain or anger released from myself,
And I held a flame to the edge of it.
And set fire to that hell.

That hell would not control me,
I would burn it thus,
To take my power back from it,
My confidence, love and trust.

On the smoke of releasing,
Things which no longer serve,
I sent them on the ethers,
To the light to restore my verve.

Janine Palmer (Silver Moon)

The Doctor

Ultimately the doctor,
Is really the inner you,
The greater vibrational wisdom,
Which balances what you do.

It's about how you process and release,
The things you appear to go through,
Which means more on deeper levels,
Than your conscious mind ever knew.

It's important not to allow your thoughts remain,
In lower vibrations of pain and loss,
Because your forward spiritual ascension,
Would be the terrible cost.

Your inner doctor knows,
You must release guilt and shame and fear,
Release sadness, resentment and unforgiveness,
And your vision will become clear.

Your inner doctor is your higher sub-consciousness,
Of which your conscious mind is unaware,
Because you are sifting through constant illusions,
And your healing won't happen there.

Your healing will come from detaching,
From your limiting ideas about so many things,
From letting go of the pain or guilt you carry,
And forgiving yourself from within.

Janine Palmer (Silver Moon)

Ancestor's Inner Warrior

The warrior did not understand,
How the balance could be torn asunder,
How the divinity he had once known,
Could be so carelessly ripped from his brothers.

He went to visit the shaman,
The medicine man of the wisdom of the ancient ways,
Who could see past this illusionary veil,
To higher truths through darkness's haze.

The shaman explained about balance,
A state which had been lost,
He also explained that good things come from the bad,
That new blessings would come from pain and loss.

He explained about initiations,
The gauntlets that warrior's must face,
To become stronger and to learn to rise above,
To return to their natural state of grace.

He explained how many things in this realm,
Are not as they appear,
And we must search for deeper meaning,
For things to become more clear.

We must now create good things,
From the ashes of the painful experiences and loss,
We must learn how to heal in the fires of rebirth,
To see beyond the din and the dross.

He said we must learn to heal ourselves and others,
And not exist in a state of unforgiveness and hate,
Because if we do we will find ourselves,
Stuck in agony at misery's gate.

We have the power and the key,
To walk out of the gates of hell,
But we must disconnect from our thoughts about things,
We must be still enough to hear the tones of the rattle and bell.

We must listen to the whispers of the ancestors,
When we hold onto pain we honor them not,
They are depending upon us to rise above,
To our divinity which we seem to have forgotten.

The ancestors need us to rise above,
So that they can rise above as well,
And we cannot do that from a negative place,
Of clinging to anger and resentment's dark hell.

Let go of the anger of past atrocities,
In order to honor them thus,
How can we now create something positive?
By clearing away old cobwebs and dark rust.

Send prayers of love and healing,
To the ancestors up with the smoke,
Honoring how they bravely paved the way,
For the power of the words now spoken.

Open the doors of unanswered questions,
To see what treasures they now hold,
To reconnect to the strength of your power,
With your inner warrior, pure and bold.

A'ho and Amen

Janine Palmer (Silver Moon)

Ancestor's Pain – Ghosts and Bones

It's horrific to think about and remember,
What some of our ancestors endured,
The holocausts and genocides,
Creating deep wounds needing to be cured.

The talking stick is in my hand,
My guides wish me to speak,
To share messages and tools for healing,
For the ascension our ancestor's seek.

Our loved ones who left this plane,
Who watch over our work now here,
They want us to be cleansed and healed,
By the power of our sacred tears.

Holding onto our anger,
Which can be a type of fuel,
But if used to keep us stuck in negativity,
We might be playing the part of the fool.

Holding onto any anger,
And sadness keeps us trapped,
It keeps the pain alive in hell,
Like a knife stuck in their back.

And every time we bring it up,
In seeking blame and rage,
Is another day an ancestor cannot,
Move forward and turn the page.

And every time we are triggered,
Our ego has its way,
And then we take two steps backwards,
Not living in the now today.

Who wants to stay stuck in hell?
When we can learn to heal and walk out?
With our warrior heads held high and proud,
With love and a victorious shout.

We are meant to ascend form this lower realm,
But we can't do it when we are stuck in hate,
We heal with love and raise them with forgiveness,
As we walk through the warrior's gate.

Those who are prisoners to their anger,
Are definitely not warriors here,
They haven't yet reached that level,
Because of darkness's veil they don't see very clear.

If you don't believe the truth of these words,
Consult a shaman or an elder anywhere,
For higher guidance above any judgment,
And for the ancestor's wisdom they share.

The shaman can help heal past-life wounds,
The elders are there with wisdom to guide,
And behind no more masks or unhealed pain,
Should any warrior continue to hide.

Pull the knife out of your ancestor's backs,
By pulling it out of your own,
Stop twisting it and feeding darkness with rage,
For which our ancestors must atone.

Don't keep them stuck in any realm,
Because you will not release,
The atrocities they want and need to be healed from,
Release them from their grief.

When any loved one passes on,
To another realm or dimension,
They can't move forward in peace and grace,
If our grief rules our action or intention.

Our grief must be released to the light,
Our grief must run its course and heal,
If it doesn't then it's the ancestor's happiness,
We unknowingly begin to steal.

In higher realms they gain pure knowledge,
For the purpose of things unknown here,
They exist in a place free of negativity,
And don't hold grudges there my dear.

But in between the realms,
Some might be restless and confused,
Because they were too attached to the physical,
And unhealed emotions so abused.

So let's not keep their pain alive,
Let us heal them now with love,
Let our energy flow from the Great Spirit,
On the wings of the raven and the dove.

Let the energy we share with the world,
Be a source of positive grace,
So if we concentrate really hard,
We will see smiles upon our ancestor's faces.

The ghosts might be the spirits,
Restless or at peace,
Depending on our actions and evolvement here,
Whether we are in prison or are released.

The ghosts might be the memories,
The whispers of the past,
Which are partial interpretations,
Based on limited information first and last.

The bones which lay in the ground,
Or scattered around as ash,
Are the remnants of the clothes they wore,
When they volunteered for their tasks.

The bones are always temporary,
It is the spirit and soul which matter,
And spirit or soul can remain stuck in unrest,
By our negative, earthly ego chatter.

Wanting revenge against ideologies,
Is the devil having his way,
The darkness which created the atrocities,
Which we keep alive when we do not slay.

To stand in our power we must forgive,
Because to forgive is to set ourselves and them free,
That is when we become a true warrior,
And it's our spirit which can then clearly see.

Our ancestors are always part of us,
And we are part of them,
And we continue to heal as a collective,
When we allow love to flow out and in.

Peace and Blessings. A'ho.

Janine Palmer (Spirit Silver Moon)

Collective healing

The soul is a spark of infinite love,
Of the sacred flame of the divine,
Who fuels the radiant ember of that love?
The love we all share which is yours and mine.

We fuel it when we share it,
It's fueled when we accept love too,
It's fueled by things which speak to our soul,
And when we allow it to come through.

It's fueled when we allow healing in,
It's fueled when we release,
The things which no longer serve us,
It's fueled when we rise above belief.

It's fueled when we discover inner truth,
When we connect to the kingdom within,
It's fueled when we connect with divine knowing,
And rise above false illusions of sin.

And sometimes when life beats us down,
And the spark of our soul's glow is dim,
Sometimes it might be an angel or a guide,
Who tends it with love until we can rise again.

And in gratitude we should stand,
And in gratitude we should pray,
In thankfulness and in light and grace,
To those beings who guide our way.

Those beings of love ever with us,
Those beings our eyes cannot see,
Those beings who whisper love in our ears,
While we rise back home to Thee.

Janine Palmer (Silver Moon)

From the Spirit

Healing flows from the spirit,
Healing comes from the body here,
Healing comes from restoring balance,
By surrender, acceptance and becoming more clear.

By clearing away the old,
The things which no longer serve,
To restore your divine glow,
To nurture your radiant energy's verve.

To imbibe from the well of forgiveness,
For others but mostly for yourself,
With the strength to disengage any part of you,
From any perception of hell.

To reconnect with divine love,
To send the needed love of divinity directly to yourself,
From and to the core of your Sacred Heart,
And from the highest Source as well.

Janine Palmer (Silver Moon)

Ascension & Spiritual Alchemy

Crumbling Falsehoods

The inner walls of my ignorance,
Were crumbling all around,
But they crumbled in a quiet way,
Only I could hear the sound.

The sound of it came out of me,
It sprang forth from my voice,
With a message my brothers and sisters,
That everyone has a choice.

What flows through my very being,
Is ancient wisdom from on high,
To break free from your programming,
And emit the Warrior's cry.

Follow not, my brothers,
What societies and religions teach,
Look within your inner kingdom,
And teach yourself to think.

Study what you think you know,
Don't follow them like sheep,
There are deeper truths undiscovered yet,
When you awaken from your sleep.

Like a glorious morning sunrise,
Casting light into the dark,
Igniting the inner flame in you,
Which starts with a tiny spark.

It's like someone removing a blindfold,
It's like finally beginning to hear,
It's like the secrets of the cosmos,
Are contained in the tiniest tear.

Allow your heart to open,
Throw the door to it open wide,
Clear out any old programming,
Of an overly conditioned mind.

Sweep out the cobwebs of patterns and habits,
Which no longer serve,
Embrace the wonder of your higher self,
And the collective consciousness verve.

Surround yourself with light and love,
Become your very own guide,
Shed and burn your dogmatic box,
It's no longer where you hide.

Listen to your guides and angels,
Be quiet and you shall hear,
Whispers from your Creator,
Which are understood and clear.

Your temple is inside yourself,
You will find it nowhere else,
Your creator ever resides there,
And your savior is yourself.

Janine Palmer (Silver Moon)

The Sword

The whispers of her footsteps,
Floated across the ground,
Stories for those who were listening,
Answers to be found.

The energy of ancient love,
Which dances in and out,
Through our memories and our awareness,
Like mists and wispy clouds.

Knowledge wraps all around us,
And some of it sinks in,
But it's so difficult to decipher,
Amongst the rattle of the din.

Whispers of his love for me,
From ages long ago,
And from current waves of energy,
Will make their presence known.

The feel of his love tickles my heart,
And make it leap with joy,
A fleeting of something words can't describe,
A glimpse of him as a boy.

The magnetic pull of his knowing gaze,
His soul called to mine from that space,
His energy pulled me to him,
And whisked me through that gate.

He gave me a sword to carry,
A sword representing the light,
He said, "You'll remember when the time is right,
To guide them in from the dark of night".

He told me I am a guardian,
He told me I am a guide,
He told me I am a messenger,
And my light I cannot hide.

He told me to help heal those with ears,
Those who were ready to hear,
He told me to share my compassionate flame,
To help them rise out of their fear.

He told me I would draw in,
The love I share from the All,
He told me we are all healing,
The damage which came from the fall.

He showed me with his mighty love,
A warrior through and through,
He said we were cut from the same cloth,
And our sparkle would imbue.

I am thankful for the depth of his love,
As he surrounds me in his care,
And as we give so shall we receive,
An abundance of blessings there.

Janine Palmer (Silver Moon)

Sacred Breeze

He was a rugged man pure of heart,
He was a quiet and beautiful soul,
He like delving into the Mysteries,
Because he enjoyed their ancient glow.

He wandered the hills and mountains,
He spoke to the trees and the streams,
He listened to the ancestor's spirits,
Who often appeared in his dreams.

They were teaching him things he'd forgotten,
Things which were so clouded due to the veil,
Deeper truths and wisdom within him,
It order for his soul to prevail.

Because we are tested in earth school,
We must learn to compromise, understand and forgive,
We must learn about surrender and acceptance,
While standing strong in order to live.

We must learn that no one controls us,
To ideas we do not bow,
No one else's truth is our own,
We must rebirth our Self here somehow.

Sometimes its hardship which does it,
Sometimes the pain which brings us to our knees,
Something rocks us and cracks us open,
And soon we feel the light of the sacred breeze.

He came across a maiden,
Who lived in seclusion by herself,
She said had walked through sacred fire,
When she disengaged from man's hell.

She was such an interesting teacher,
She walked in a level of grace,
Her eyes glowed with eternity's fire,
So beautiful the smile on her face.

They shared a depth of connection,
Neither had found with anyone else,
They understood the benefit,
Of sharing from their higher Self.

From then on they walked together,
They were teachers in their land,
They were healers in touch with the Mystery,
In their own strength they continued to stand.

Janine Palmer (Silver Moon)

Janine Palmer (Silver Moon) ChT

Pieces of her Soul

Along the winding paths,
Of so many journeys before,
She left pieces of her soul behind,
Through many opening and closing of doors.

But it was time to retrieve them,
So she went into the woods,
She drew a circle around her,
And in the middle of it she stood.

She called in her guides and her angels,
And she knelt down on her knees,
She asked them to help her call her power back,
And she asked for help from the trees.

She thanked the Highest Divinity,
For the gift of love, I Am,
And she called her power back,
From any woman or any man.

She called back her power from anyone,
Any of her power needing to be freed,
And she returned any power she was holding,
Which needed to be set free.

She sat in a place of forgiveness,
First and foremost she forgave herself,
She released herself from her self-made prison,
And released herself from hell.

She forgave every person she could think of,
Any perception she had of harm or ill will,
She forgave them for their trespasses,
Whether intended or not, she forgave them and was still.

She called back any pieces,
Of her soul she had left behind,
Which restored her spiritual vision,
Which due to the veil had been blind.

She built a little fire,
And negative karma she threw in,
She threw in the falsehoods she had carried,
She threw in the illusion of sin.

Sin is not a part of her,
Because she is a divine creation of God,
And it was high time she broke free of the lies,
Which for centuries have been taught.

She lifted the dark veil of dogma,
And she threw it into the fire,
And as she freed herself from dark falsehoods,
Her spirit was lifted higher.

She came to full recognition,
She is a co—creator with God,
And along these pathways of illusions,
No longer would she trod.

She stood in gratitude among the trees,
She stood with her angels and guides,
And now that she had burned her masks,
No longer must she hide.

She is here to speak of fairy tales,
Because in that kingdom far, far away,
She found the pieces of her soul
Which she'd lost in other days.

Janine Palmer (Silver Moon)

It's Only a Test

It's only ever a test,
Of mind and heart and soul,
It's to test your strength and mettle,
Breaking through the veil, the goal.

We are tested on many levels,
An ongoing cosmic parade,
To see what you'll create with your free will,
And the results of choices made.

What roles do we play?
What masks do we wear?
When do we disengage from falsehoods?
When do we climb Ascension's stairs?

We pass the tests when we rise above,
When we move in flow and grace,
When we remove our masks and recognize,
The beauty of our true face.

Recognize the tests and learn from them,
Serve others as you go,
Shine your light in the darkness,
And let your beauty glow.

Janine Palmer (Silver Moon)

Higher Self & The Dream

What of saints and angels,
And how they look after man?
What about the knowledge of Scripture,
Which points to a line in the sand?

Beyond the line which man draws,
Is a place inside the Self,
And within the higher self,
Is where the Creator dwells.

How beautiful it is,
When a man or woman discovers within,
The kingdom of heaven, the temple,
Where their true awakening begins.

To reconnect with the sacred place,
Of love housed by every soul,
A delightful reunion of sacred space,
More holy than you know.

The conscious mind cannot fathom,
The deeper part of spirit,
But the higher self is well aware,
And ever does it hear it.

The higher self is well aware,
Of knowledge over millennia gained,
And of the sacred wisdom in the hearts of men,
Secretly retained.

When the initiate is ready,
The teacher will appear,
And knowledge will prevail,
The Christ consciousness will become clear.

It is a collective consciousness,
Shared by Lord and a king,
It's here and now and all around us,
When we wake up from the dream.

Janine Palmer (Silver Moon)

Meet Me

She said, Meet me in the nether world,
Away from the dysfunction so near,
Away from illusion's obstacles,
Where nothing ever seems clear.

Take me away from the ego's lair,
Where people treat each other so badly,
Take me from this gauntlet of pain,
Where so many people seem ever so sad.

I want to be with the light of your soul,
Because your vibration reminds me of home,
I want you to hold me and never let go,
This earth plane is no place to roam.

The beauty is so intermittent,
It fluctuates in and out of the light,
People have done things to hurt me,
But I have risen above that illusional plight.

I don't care to linger here longer,
In this lower vibrational stew,
I only want to journey away,
To another dimension in the company of you.

Because I know you possess great honor,
I know you're a magical light,
I recognize your familiar vibration,
It's strong and true and bright.

I've had to walk away from the cruel ones,
They who once tread upon my heart,
They were the catalyst for the phoenix within me,
Part of my rebirth experience to start.

And before they kicked me with steel-toed boots,
They shared a love which filled my soul,
And the remnants of that love I will carry with me,
Wherever and however I go.

The love to me was such a gift,
Pieces of each are felt and adored,
Until one or the other severs that connection,
Simply by cutting the cord.

Dishonoring a being of great love,
Is dishonoring a part of your spirit's shell,
But they will experience the pain they inflicted,
So they will experience that slice of hell.

Do try and rise above ego,
And selfish pursuits on your course,
Treat others how you would have them treat you,
Unless you like the taste and feel of remorse.

He said, I'm sorry for what you have gone through,
Earth school is the warrior's field,
I will meet you in the nether realms,
Where all old pain and sadness will yield.

And that heaviness in your heart you have carried,
We will both peel it off and clear it away,
We will release it to the light to transmute it,
To never again darken your day.

And she surrounded him with an angel's light,
And he filled her bruised heart with his love every day,
He said, I shall never dishonor you, my lady,
My honor is yours and so it will stay.

Janine Palmer (Silver Moon)

Spiral

Life on this plane is not linear,
Life on this plane is a spiral,
It spirals up with experiences,
Curving around to re-test us all the while.

Something might come back around again,
To test us and our reactions now,
To see of it's healed or if it triggers us,
Do we fight it or do we bow?

Do we bow in peacefulness?
As acceptance and release has given us power,
Or do we retreat behind our old armor,
To our patterns and habit's prison tower?

Do we feel the old pain?
Do we feel the need to fight or attack?
Is it a reminder to us now?
That we still need to take our power back?

When that spiral brings us back around,
And we find we are triggered no more,
We know we have grown and evolved,
And we've ascended through another door.

The strength we gain is the purpose,
To rise above fear and illusion,
To be reacquainted with the purpose of love,
Because we rose above confusion.

To disconnect from the programming,
To come back in touch with our hearts,
Which always speaks to our soul divine,
From that love we are never apart.

Even when we don't see it,
It's asking us to further seek,
To reconnect with our divine truth,
And to strengthen what is weak.

Janine Palmer (Silver Moon)

Drum Beat

The drumbeat guides us within,
To a divine reality unseen,
To do healing work on levels,
Which serve us in between.

The drumbeat of our human hearts,
Helps guide us on our Way,
To learn to feel and to listen,
As old programs now are slayed.

The drumbeat on the sacred hide,
Calling in our master guides,
Into our higher awareness,
Where no longer do we hide.

The drumbeat of the universe,
Music created at different levels,
Different frequencies dancing,
As we rise above the devils.

Calling back our power,
Through the collective drumbeat as it sings,
Primal tones of sacred focus,
For the gifts it always brings.

The wisdom of the shaman,
Through ancestral lines,
For our healing and awakening,
As we weave through space and time.

Janine Palmer (Silver Moon)

Your Magnificence & Worthiness

Gatekeeper

Who is the mysterious gate keeper,
Who holds the elusive key?
Gaze into the looking glass, my friend
Lo and behold, it's you and me.

There are tendrils of infinite knowing,
Tickling our senses now and again,
Reminders of our divine origins,
Of the kingdom of heaven within.

There are whispers of love which wash over your soul,
There is a radiance of light so serene,
Tingling sensations wash away your fears,
Glimpses of reality break into your dream.

Embrace the soul mates who remind you,
Who challenge you to open your heart,
To remember your brilliant magnificence,
To return to where you start.

Janine Palmer (Silver Moon)

Ultimate Oblivion

The ultimate oblivion,
Like a scourge upon the earth,
Where beings of divinity,
Have forgotten their value and worth.

All because of falsehoods,
Implanted in the mind,
And because we sleep in ignorance,
We forgot about the vine.

We forgot we are all connected,
And duality is in force,
We think we're separate from our Creator,
Too focused on the dark horse.

In your heart and waiting,
For you to wake up and recognize,
Is the true light of divinity,
Which has been hidden from your sight.

It's been waiting for you to awaken,
From the fog and from the haze,
To get on your path back to the light,
Seeing clearly now out of the maze.

Open your heart to your own light,
Which is ever connected with Source,
And share your light with the world,
Which lights your brother's course.

This is the work of Ascension,
When we heal ourselves we heal the whole,
When we disconnect from the lies,
And release the pain we reach our goal.

Janine Palmer (Silver Moon)

Whispers and Shadows

She entered into the dark forest,
To hear what it had to say,
The secrets of ancient wisdom,
The art of the light-worker's way.

Some people have cause to remember,
Their ancestor's knowledge and rites,
Their intuition razor sharp,
Wisdom flowing from dimensions just out of sight.

The trees whispered to her,
'Every path leads homeward, you're never lost on your way,
You might stumble in confusion, but you will never be waylaid,
Our boughs touch the higher worlds, our roots touch infinity,
You may speak to a tree for wisdom, only to find it is also in thee.'

Trees are beautiful signposts,
In their majesty they ever direct,
To witness and absorb their beauty,
To other realms you will connect.

Trees are sanctuaries, God also resides in them,
To speak to them is to let God speak to you,
Learn how to speak to them and listen,
Truth and guidance will ever come through.

She was told through their ancient wisdom,
From the sacred beyond the din,
It's not a matter of escaping one's own suffering,
It's about rising above the illusion of sin.

It's important to recognize man's folly,
And where he has been ensnared,
To rise above falsehoods and illusion,
Our love with others must be shared.

Listen long and let them reveal mysteries,
Through their leaves rustling in the wind,
To break out of our shells and our prisons,
To let our true purpose begin.

Trees have their scars just like we do,
They are eternal like all of creation,
They remind us to guard our powerful thoughts,
Because we create our own manifestations.

They are connected to the eternal mother,
They are sparks of holy thought,
They are ever beautiful reminders,
Of so many things we forgot.

They are signposts and reminders,
To remember that we are divine,
And to let go of egoic thoughts,
Of the notion of yours and mine.

We are all connected,
We all have the very same purpose upon this earth,
To reunite with our sacred origins,
To die to the false and to our truth rebirth.

She gave gratitude to the trees for their wisdom,
Their beauty and their love,
And when she looked up into the branches,
She saw a raven and a dove.

Janine Palmer (Silver Moon)

The Lamps

What of those beings who help lost souls,
Souls who are stuck because of religion and fear,
Who didn't transition from this life due to falsehoods believed,
From ideologies taught by those too closed to hear.

From adopting ideas about hell,
Which darkness wove in to control,
And in ignorance mankind bought the lies,
Which interfere with his purpose and goal.

So many beings introduced to fear,
A program here of false power,
To allow it to have such debilitating control,
Is to prevent the growth of a flower.

So many on earth are waylaid,
They suffer and stumble in vein,
And when it's time to go home to the energy of love,
They hesitate, lost and afraid.

By being caught in the snare of darkness,
Sometimes they don't recognize their own divine love,
So Source sends beings of love and compassion to guide them,
On the spirit of hope from the dove.

We all have angels and guides,
Every soul on this path,
But not all acknowledge or open to them,
We simply have to ask.

So who are the earth angels, these seers?
The empaths and intuitives here,
Who can see, sense and hear things other cannot,
And to the lost souls they are lanterns so clear.

They are so gifted and open in love,
They have risen above fear to serve others,
To serve beings walking in between worlds,
To assist lost and confused sisters and brothers.

Walking in between worlds,
A cosmic balancing act,
To offer assistance in compassion and love,
To be the light and the hope they once lacked.

This poem is a message of gratitude,
For those earth angels whose compassion is so great,
That they take the hands of the lost souls,
And lead them back to their gates.

Janine Palmer (Spirit Silver Moon)

Find Peace in Love

He wrote ancient truths from his deepest heart,
He would bare wounded and healed parts of his soul,
He wrote on parchment and in his thoughts,
Such wisdom more precious than gold.

Because what we know and what we feel,
And what we learn upon this hellish plane,
Has far more worth and value,
Than any material thing we could gain.

The material often keeps us distracted,
To lower vibrational things,
Keeping us fully behind the veil,
In darkness where our soul does not sing.

When we recognize our magnificence,
It is not something we earn but discover,
We remember the deeper parts of us,
Which we also see it in our sisters and brothers.

One of my dear soul connections,
I've known him since ancient times,
He supports me on levels so important to me,
And he is also a master of rhymes.

He walked through hell and came out of it,
He learned to open his dear heart once more,
He learned to trust in the flow of creation,
And to always be aware of and open new doors.

One of his friends so connected with nature,
A healer of the ancient ways and knowing,
Said something powerful and profound to him,
And his answer was of the universal ways always growing.

She said, may peace, love and joy find a home
Once again within your being,
Thank you for what you share with the world,
Of the wisdom and experience from your intuitive seeing.

Because he is a seer for the greater good,
He is an intuitive, empathic and mystical guide,
Who had to learn like all of us,
From our demons we cannot hide.

We must tame them through our battles,
We must take our power back,
We must rise out of our own ashes,
We must rebirth ourselves from lack.

So his answer to his dear friend,
What he learned from the wings of the dove,
Was to tell her that he found his peace,
He said, I have found my peace in love.

He opened the door to his frozen heart,
Just a crack to let some light in,
But the light found still blazing there,
Was an invitation for new life to begin.

He was shown love by many beings,
He had encountered along his rough path,
And he accepted the love they gave him,
But he always gave it back.

Janine Palmer (Silver Moon)

Ropes

What are these ropes that bind us?
Are they connected to our thoughts about things?
Are they weights like balls and chains?
Are they like the scorpion's sting?

Are we attached to our ideas?
Are we attached to our beliefs?
Do we recognize the imposter in the midst?
Falsehood is the thief.

The falsehoods which we believe to be true,
Hold us hostage and at bay,
They keep us chained or roped or chorded,
To things which are not meant to stay.

Though ropes can always be severed,
But only when you have the power to cut through,
Only when you regain the knowledge of your divinity,
And the illusion do you finally see through.

What in the world are these fairy tales,
Which we cling to and believe?
Believing the lie that we are unworthy,
And that we need a savior to receive.

When we are our very own saviors,
Because the savior lives inside me and you,
But only when you open your heart and soul,
Will you see the light shining through.

Being closed in belief is a tragedy,
But only as long as it lasts,
It's darkness's greatest victory,
And to break free is the task.

Open my dears to your knowing,
To your inner truth, the kingdom within,
Open to you divine magnificence,
And let your ascension begin.

Janine Palmer (Silver Moon)

Love Now hidden

Tossed about like a feather,
Tossed about like a leaf,
On the streams of spirit calling,
Moving through wrath and pain and grief.

Finding love now hidden,
Between the nooks and cracks,
In unexpected places,
Filling in us what we lack.

And he or she will come along,
Like a beacon her on our path,
To guide us and share their wisdom,
To help bring remembrance back.

To help us recall our worthiness,
To help us reconnect with grace,
To wipe away the occasional tears,
When trickle down our face.

To guide and to lift us,
Sometimes rough and sometimes soft,
To reconnect us to you inner truth,
Which is only temporarily lost.

And the love we feel and the love we share,
By far the greatest treasure on earth,
And what we do with the wisdom gained,
Is part of our rebirth.

Janine Palmer (Silver Moon)

Flowers or Weeds

It's greener where you water it,
Whether it's good or bad,
Whether you water weeds or flowers,
Whether you dwell in happy or sad.

What you give your attention to,
From that energy you will grow,
Is it positive or is it negative?
Does it block you or does it flow?

Although we all need the negative to teach us,
We learn from the contrast between the two,
To know the difference and rise above,
To our higher self where love comes through.

Do you take your power back?
Or do you give it away?
Do you release old burdens frequently?
Or do you allow them to stay?

Are you a friend of forgiveness?
Do you use it as a healing tool?
Or do you cling to a victim's resentment?
Which wears the hat of a fool.

Because when we identify with victim mentality,
We simply give our power away,
We attach to ourselves a label,
Which is rather like a grave.

To lie in a grave with no power,
Alive but living not,
Waiting in expectation for someone else to save you,
Means your magnificence you forgot.

Are you more of a flower or more of a weed?
And which do you water more thus?
Do you oil the hinges on the door to your heart?
Or do you allow it to sit and rust?

Your thoughts create your reality,
Do you think of flowers or do you think of weeds?
Do you serve your brother on your journey?
Is your life affected positively or negatively by your deeds?

Do you hear the strength of your voice?
Do you use it for good purpose and power?
Do you live in a bed of weeds, my dear?
Or in a bed of glorious flowers?

Janine Palmer (Spirit Silver Moon)

Blessed Be Our Magic

Do You Feel Nature?

What do you find in nature?
What speaks fondly to your soul?
What do you do to gain knowledge?
What nurtures you soul and makes your heart glow?

Do you wonder at the beauty of a babbling brook?
The way the water meanders through the creek?
The magnificence of a waterfall and how it draws you in?
Or the feeling of serenity and peace?

Do you listen to the sound of the wind?
As it whispers through the trees?
Do you sit in their regal presence?
And give thanks for all of these?

Do you enjoy the shade of the lofty trees?
Or the color as their autumn leaves turn?
Do you like to watch wild animals in them?
For their primal beauty do you yearn?

Do you listen when nature speaks?
Do you feel the energy radiating from the earth?
Do you feel stresses melting away?
Do you feel your own roots to her?

Janine Palmer (Silver Moon)

Nature's Beauty Speaks

Though I know not the names of the trees,
Which continue to beckon me there,
A fondness exists for their sheltering warmth,
In winter or summer so fair.

What a delight the transition to witness,
The changing seasons as they arrive,
The beauty of nature's display,
The stages in which life thrives.

Oh the harmony of ancient things,
Which whisper in the wind,
Their essence evident in their presence,
Appreciation and adoration the blend.

Stately stones still standing,
After hundreds and hundreds of years,
Cared for by tender hands and hearts,
And blood and sweat and tears.

Through the dedicated and the faithful,
This came to be yours and mine,
To care for with the gentlest hand,
To hand down these treasures so fine.

Janine Palmer (Silver Moon)

Dancing Shadows

Shadows dance round standing stones, or is it really light?
It matters not what casts the shadows, be it day or night,
She came under cover of darkness, with hooded cloak in place,
The clouds obscuring the moon, hid the look upon his face.

There she stood, his beauty, from ancient days gone by,
His enchanting little goddess, bending light beams from on high,
She left a trail of light divine, upon the beloved ground,
When he encountered this complex being, his purpose had been found.

She spoke to him without words, she spoke to him with her eyes,
She was as mysterious as the mists, her purpose in disguise,
She was a mixture of two lovely birds, the raven and the dove,
Dark and light always swirling, as below, so above.

The compassion from her deepest heart, he loved that sacred space,
Her glowing light was a brilliant flame, in anger or in grace,
Bridges had been crossed, from dimensions of sacred light,
But the path is never easy, navigating the dark of night.

Weaving bridges of light, for creatures great and small,
Sharing God's deepest love, creating balance and healing for all,
Her heart is filled with a gratitude, which she cannot put into words,
That he appeared on her lonely path, her sacred prayer was heard.

He sees into the very depths of her ancient and mystical soul,
She's the sacred target, he's the archer who's mastered his bow;
His spirit sings so deeply to her, she remembers their soul's connection,
In each other's hearts, they see each other's reflection.

He gathers her to him gently, at night in the swirling mists,
They are surrounded by angel's wings and blessed with the angel's kiss,
They recognize their calling, they remember other journeys before,
They are ready to venture hand and hand as they walk through another door.

Janine Palmer (Silver Moon)

Thanks and Blessings

Life continued to hand me,
A number of challenging tests,
I learned I couldn't hold things against myself,
If I wanted to be my best.

I have to thank love for the pleasure,
I have to thank love for the pain,
I thank wisdom and my mind for turning,
So many losses to gains.

I thank my heart for learning forgiveness,
For loving and letting go,
I thank my soul for recognizing,
I am on my path to help me grow.

My thanks go out to those,
Who recognized the light in me,
And for showing me hidden beauty within,
And aspects I didn't see.

My soul mates have been good teachers,
And I have learned restraint,
Whether they shared their love or caused me pain,
Reuniting with them was great.

What are blessings anyway?
Don't they often come to us in disguise?
The old must fall away to make room for the new,
Life is about surprise.

I AM thankful for great blessings,
Which have arrived in so many ways,
People and experiences, wisdom and knowledge,
Gleaned from new gifts every day.

Thank you to the higher power,
Which we all come from, our beloved Source,
And for the love we show to others,
Who come back to us of course.

Janine Palmer (Silver Moon)

Through the Trees

Through the trees there's always more,
Don't they point the way?
Are you aware of their infinite wisdom,
Do you hear what they have to say?

To hear, first you must listen,
Listen to wisdom speak,
Listen to the babbling Brook,
The whispers of the creek.

Listen to the squirrels,
Listen to the birds,
Listen to the stories on the wind,
And tell me what you heard.

Do you hear your grandfathers' whispers?
Do you hear your grandmothers' words?
They whisper to you through many things,
I wonder have you heard.

Will you teach your children,
To listen to the trees?
Will you teach them to dance in the rain?
Or to feel the spirit of the breeze?

Janine Palmer (Silver Moon)

In the Company of the Trees

In the magic of the forest,
In the energy of wisdom fair,
Was the secret dwelling place of the lady,
Beside the lake there was her lair.

The place where divine energy swirled,
In a vortex of infinite light,
With the trees which anchored heaven and earth,
Through the sun by day and the moon by night.

She was so many things wrapped up in one,
She was an extension of a great soul,
A healer and a messenger here,
For the greater good of humanity's goal.

Some people were not quite ready,
For what she was here to teach,
Some people were too afraid to step out of their boxes,
And for higher awareness now to reach.

The trees they spoke her language,
They spoke to the heart of her spirit,
They whispered their ancient wisdom,
And she was open enough to hear it.

She existed in the lush beauty there,
In the company of the trees,
Because nothing else for her could compare,
They were her greatest gifts and her soul they did please.

They circled her in protection,
And a fire burned in the center,
And those of pure hearts and souls on earth,
Were always welcome to enter.

She shared healing words and comfort,
The wisdom from ancient days,
With anyone open to hear it,
As they navigated life's challenging maze.

The animals were constant visitors,
Whether in spirit of in physical form,
They were guides and wisdom keepers,
Who helped humanity weather the storms.

And the days the skies were cloudy,
And the days the rains would come,
Were the days she cherished most of all,
For the lush emerald green which nature spun.

And her unconditional lover,
Would place flowers in her hair,
He would hold her closely every night,
In the magic of her lair.

Janine Palmer (Silver Moon)

Trees and Stones

The trees possess great beauty,
No words here could describe,
Their fragrance and healing energy,
In gratitude I imbibe.

They are pillars of such great strength,
They carry the wisdom of the ages,
Their branches and roots anchor heaven and earth,
They are gentle and quiet sages.

The stones emit healing energies,
Different vibrations and they glow,
Their colors so brilliant call to us,
Different levels of connectedness they show.

The trees and the stones work together,
They sing if only we could hear,
And if you ask them for healing and guidance,
To higher knowing your path they will steer.

Janine Palmer (Silver Moon)

Feathers

Feathers are used for healing,
Feathers are used for flight,
Feathers are used to clear away the negative,
Feathers are messages from angels bright.

Some feathers create a certain sound,
Some feathers are silent in the night,
Some feathers when found might cheer us,
Some feathers redirect us from wrong to right.

Feathers are used for ceremonies,
Feathers are given as gifts,
Feathers are used as medicine,
In and out of dimensions they shift.

Feathers might carry a shape shifter,
In and out of another realm of majesty,
A higher vibration of the chameleon totem,
To enable the shaman to see.

He or she experiences a different reality,
From the perspective of a great bird,
And wisdom from other dimensions,
Is known, experienced and heard.

But a being must be open,
To be guided by the ancestor's hand,
And the simple gift of wayward feather,
Might be a profound message where we stand.

A'ho

Janine Palmer (Silver Moon)

Under the Wolf Moon

She went to the woods one evening,
To listen to the trees,
To walk through the moonlit shadows,
And hear their whispers on the breeze.

As she walked the peaceful forest path,
She came upon him in a clearing there,
Standing there staring up at the moon,
The moonlight glistening off his hair.

He turned in surprise to look at her,
Then he looked up at the moon again,
His light hair halfway down his back,
She wondered if she should retreat then.

She felt there was no threat from him,
And he said, "Did you come to see the Wolf Moon?"
She said, "No I was just taking a walk,"
He said, "I hope you don't leave too soon."

She took a chance and approached him,
And he turned and smiled at her now,
She introduced herself as Charlotte,
And he bent and gave her a bow.

He told her his name was Liam,
He said he loved the moonlit nights,
He said there was nothing quite like the energy,
Of the silvery, mystical light.

She stood with him there under the moon,
And felt the energy of the rays,
And she felt a comforting tingling sensation come over her,
Whispering of magical ways.

He told her magic is all around you,
Magic is everywhere,
Magic is in your heart and soul,
And it lifts us when we share.

Before the night was over,
After they had talked for hours on end,
They danced together in the moonlight,
And they felt the magic between them blend.

Under the wolf moon she found magic,
She found that the magic resided within,
And when she opened to it and let it out,
New opportunities would begin.

Janine Palmer (Silver Moon)

Fully Blessed

It matters not what time in history,
That man had a message to share,
That man had a higher knowing,
That mankind has something to bear.

That internal bliss was an ancient guide,
Which lighted his way in the dark,
That his heart was his trusted friend,
That he discovered his tiny God spark.

When he discovered the error of judgment,
When he embraced the necessity of love,
When he accepted the light and the shadow,
Like the wings of the Raven and Dove.

When he breathed in so deeply divine love,
When he breathed all fear out of his chest,
When he remembered his true divinity,
He realized he was fully blessed.

Janine Palmer (Silver Moon)

The Breath of Love

She journeyed into the dark woods,
Which were really full of light,
She connected with ancient wisdom there,
And the breath of love so bright.

The breath and the spirit of the love of God,
The Father/Mother Divine,
Who were always with her even when she forgot,
Through this illusion of space and time.

And the work she did here for the collective,
From the compassion of the Ancient of Days,
The glorious light of her soul divine,
As we all navigate this curious maze.

A goddess here for the people,
So many of them here unknown,
Until they share the light of their spirit,
When compassion and healing are shown.

But they are also warriors,
They have to navigate the fall out of pain,
Of misunderstanding and persecution,
While their important callings they maintain.

Some beings shared love with her for periods of time,
Until their egos reared their heads,
And then she had to disconnect,
From the vibration of the spiritually dead.

When we listen to ego's foul drama,
And disconnect from the spirit's light,
Is when we find ourselves in strife and struggle,
Periods of the soul's dark night.

When we dishonor a brother or sister,
In selfishness, ignorance or fear,
When we create pain in the heart of an angel,
We will experience the feelings which created those tears.

She entered the woods for the healing she needed,
To keep herself grounded to needed levels of love,
And to hear the whispers of guidance waiting there,
From the raven and the dove.

She thanked the trees for their wisdom,
For their beauty and guidance too,
For the healing energy they freely shared,
When she allowed it to come through.

She thanked her guides, the many,
The Ascended Masters and animals around,
The angels who are there for us all,
In quiet reverence they ever abound.

The beings unseen around her there,
Who lifted her when this life wore her down,
When she needed some laughter or a kind of love,
In nature and in pure hearts is where it's found.

Janine Palmer (Silver Moon)

Your Own Honor

Second Sight

Through familiar grooves and patterns,
We know not what we create,
It becomes ever more difficult to find,
The keyhole to the light, the gate.

We identify too much with things,
Which are external to ourselves,
When it's into the mystery within us,
Which we should ever endeavor to delve.

There are so many questions marks,
Wet upon life's mysterious page,
Dark bundles to sort through daily,
Of confusion, sadness, fear and rage.

Lo, an invitation for the curious,
To take a step within,
To find that pinhole of eternal light,
Sheltered from external din.

A choice to remain stubborn and shuttered,
Bound in incomprehension,
Or to embrace the Oneness within,
Apart as it is from deception.

The cause and the perpetrator,
Are part of the ongoing dream,
Brilliant lights and ciphers,
Of the collective conscious stream.

The cause and the perpetrator,
And the victim as well,
Caught up in the illusion,
Of their own private little hell.

Can you countenance this?
This erroneous, demanding need?
Or will you disengage from it,
And from the light stream feed?

Illusions and misinterpretations of facts,
Eroding minds and families in lack,
Or pulling off the cloak of lies,
And getting your connection to your creator back.

No more identifying with the dark and dull,
Your heart is free and light,
A surge of your very own energy returns,
And you regain your second sight.

Janine Palmer (Silver Moon)

In Gratitude and Release, the Rose

She stood in the woods for answers,
She went to find clarity there,
She went in search of healing from the trees,
Where her heart and soul she laid bare.

She gave thanks to the Creator,
She gave thanks to the earth and the trees,
She gave thanks for all her blessings,
And the interesting path she continued to weave.

On her knees in prayer and surrender,
She had a vision of a guide,
Who handed her a single rose,
And said it was time for her tears to be dried.

He told her to place any type of burden,
Any type of fear, hesitation or doubt,
Into the rose and release it,
To the angels waiting in the clouds.

She released what did not serve her,
She carried the burdens no more,
She released the rose to the light divine,
To move forward in God's love forevermore.

Janine Palmer (Silver Moon)

Star Gate

Even though there were beings who loved her,
They understood not her mysterious depth,
They looked on in helpless confusion,
So many times when she wept.

But through life's delightful trials,
She began to open to herself,
She experienced expanding and awakening consciousness,
And realized she could walk out of hell.

She was a messenger and a teacher,
And to some it was just ramblings,
But she was also a compassionate healer,
And so many experienced levels of healing.

For the greater good she was a most gracious host,
She was the mystery of the ancients, here to clear away the ghosts,
She came to remind herself and others in their power to be strong,
Because reminding us of love and light is her siren's song.

She is a weaver of words and wisdom,
Here to wake them from their sleep,
For healing from false illusions,
Which cause so many to weep.

I speak of the Divine Feminine,
Half of the Creative Force,
The nurturing pitcher of compassion,
So long ignored on humanity's course.

Oh the fragrance of her luminous flower,
So intoxicating when it begins to bloom,
Because she is here to weave the love back in,
Since they took away her loom.

She wants you to remember your magnificence,
She encourages that any old dross you now burn,
In order to rise from those ashes,
Because you are remembering truth when you learn.

Janine Palmer (Silver Moon)

Rewrite Your Addiction

Perhaps your addiction occurred to teach you,
The powerful lesson of rising above,
Of not letting something have control over you,
To peel away that illusionary glove.

That deceptive disguise you hide behind,
Trying to numb and mask the pain,
Because it's buried there inside of you,
Where you allow it to remain.

What if you no longer claimed them?
The addiction and the pain,
Release them from your being,
So in hell you won't remain.

Make it no longer 'your' addiction,
Because it doesn't really belong to you,
It's only a signpost to point you,
To another way to get through.

Perhaps you wrote in that addiction,
To your soul contract to experience regaining your strength,
But you have the power to re-write your addiction,
It's doesn't need to linger at length.

Honor the self you buried,
Underneath those illusions and thoughts,
Allow those caged birds to fly free,
Because you really own them not.

Set them free and fill that space,
With love for yourself from the divine,
Be prepared to walk through the new doors which will open,
And know that everything will be fine.

Janine Palmer (Silver Moon)

Detachment

There is a power in detachment,
To take a step back from illusion's false show,
To detach from the hell you or others create,
Which dims the light of the soul.

Attachment causes us suffering,
As the Buddha did so teach,
And it sucks our life force energy,
Like any unwanted leach.

But if and when we can learn to detach,
If only to a degree,
Then as an observer of limited perspective,
From a different angle we can see.

And from a bit of a distance,
We can begin to find peace and calm,
To stop resisting what seems to persist,
And in our own power we will find sweet balm.

The only power they can take from us,
It the power by reaction we give,
This journey is to teach us strength and wisdom,
Sometimes we die a little and sometimes we live.

Detachment is taking your power back,
Detachment will help you reflect,
About how and to whom you give your power away,
And what thoughts you will welcome and which you'll reject.

It's important to be aware of programs,
Which keep us in a type of dysfunctional loop,
When we break free of that with will and intention,
New blessings can come through.

Janine Palmer (Silver Moon)

Mirror, Mirror

Mirror of Forgiveness

In a dream she entered a garden,
To forgive people for their perceived wrongs,
To rise above the hurtful things they did,
To listen to her heart's sacred song.

In this garden sometimes were angels,
In this garden were sometimes guides,
There to help her heal and release,
Blocks stuck which liked to hide.

A guide in the garden greeted her,
And had her stand before a mirror,
To say the name of whomever she was forgiving,
To see if it was clear.

When she spoke the words of forgiveness,
Of the person with their name,
She was to observe whether any image of them lingered there,
It was time to step away from their blame.

If an image of them still lingered there,
There might still be more to forgive,
But if it was only her image staring back,
It was time to move on and live.

Feelings of closeness often change,
Due to so many differing perceptions,
And when old pain comes out to wound,
One might retreat from it and the other might feel rejection.

We don't often realize our treatment of others,
Some won't seem to take responsibility for their actions,
Twisting their issues and firing them like weapons,
Will always cause or create reactions.

If a person has the self-respect,
And if a person has the strength,
They might need to detach and walk away,
From projectiles created by or creating grief.

With the act of true forgiveness from love,
Certain karma is balanced and done,
And from illusions and merry-go-rounds,
We are no longer drawn to nor do we run.

To stand in our truth and acceptance,
Of who we know we really are,
To have the courage to walk away from what we know is untrue,
Is to avoid the inflicting of many new scars.

The mirror in the garden,
The mirror of the dream,
Will show us the truth when we are ready,
When in acceptance and love we glean.

Janine Palmer (Silver Moon)

Merlin's Beard

People and situations are mirrors,
Reflecting back what we need to see,
A new perspective and a new awareness,
Of how we do or do not want to be.

The fire which purifies denser energy,
Cleanses our temple, sweeping the floor,
There is magic within waiting to ignite,
If only we would love ourselves more.

From beneath the hood you might glimpse,
Fragments which glow from your mantle,
You're a wizard or a warrior and life's field,
You can see Merlin's beard in a candle.

Your divine light is like a candle,
And many other lights are lit by yours,
By sharing compassion, warmth and knowledge,
Your wisdom then creates its own course.

Are you separate, then, from your neighbor?
Hell no, if you would only but see,
The illusion is the lower self or little "I",
The divine reality is the "we".

Janine Palmer (Silver Moon)

Remedy

The remedy to anything,
Is in your very hands,
When you disconnect from doubt and fear,
And in your truth you stand.

You have the power to heal,
Connected as you are to Source,
You come from the most amazing love,
Your divinity of course.

Open a space for healing,
And then invite it in,
Release any cumbersome burdens,
And let the healing begin.

You may call in your angels,
To assist you in the endeavor,
Release what no longer serves you,
Negative ties do sever.

It is very important,
That you hold nothing against yourself,
Connect to your Higher Self,
For direction, support and help.

The remedy is in detaching,
From things which hold you back,
Disconnecting from programming and falsehoods,
There is nothing which you lack.

Be thankful for your blessings,
And watch as they do grow,
Be open to learn new things,
There is so much you don't know.

Open your heart in wonder,
And allow yourself to be filled,
With love and light from all around,
Your sacred fallow field.

Janine Palmer (Silver Moon)

Souls

We might feel a deep connection,
To a being we cannot explain,
We should trust out heart and our instincts,
To receive blessings to be gained.

We come to each other for reasons,
Gifts at first not explained,
Things agreed upon before we came here,
They are lessons preordained.

There are gifts which become lessons,
And lessons which become gifts,
There are choices, decisions and variables,
Floating around in the mists.

We are very complex beings,
Our beauty, our gifts, our light,
When we open and trust and move with the flow,
We connect with our second sight.

Our deeper sight of seeing,
Not with our physical eyes,
Of seeing another's true beauty,
Which is seeing beyond the guise.

When we see past so many illusions,
To the beauty and light within,
We rise above misperceptions,
Of the erroneous belief in sin (and our true path can begin).

Janine Palmer (Silver Moon)

Spirit Wind

I AM elusive like the wind,
I AM spirit whispering in the breeze,
I AM gratitude, love and compassion,
And with others I share these.

I AM a delicate mixture,
Of the shadow and the light,
The love from my compassionate flame,
Glows strong and true and bright.

I descended to this earth school,
To share God's love divine,
Whispers of higher wisdom speak,
To me from the ethers so fine.

The Tree of Life is ascending,
It's growing on so many levels,
It grows in beauty and grace,
When mankind rises above devils.

Spirit whispers to me,
Of God's love everywhere,
And I AM called by the Holy Spirit,
God's messages I must share.

I would encourage you to release,
Anything you hold against yourself,
Open your heart and soul to healing,
And know all will be well.

Janine Palmer (Silver Moon)

Light

Don't withhold your light due to old pain,
Don't hold to that poison so vile,
Give all your old pain to the light,
Lighten your heart as you learn from each trial.

Who is the being who speaks to your heart?
Who shows you the love you need?
Do you honor their pureness of spirit?
Do you heal them or make their heart bleed?

Honor the Father, the Spirit, the Son,
Honor the people, the chosen ones,
Honor their love, their kindness, their soul,
Tell them what they deserve to know.

When you share love and kindness, when you rise out of your pain,
Do you experience the effects of Grace?
That's God working through you to heal another,
And you heal yourself in that space.

When we cannot extend in kindness,
Our hand to another in need,
We are a prisoner of our own pain,
From which we desperately need to be freed.

No one can do it for us,
We are our jailer and we hold the key,
How we treat others we treat ourselves,
How do we set ourselves free?

Hold nothing against yourself,
Hold nothing against anyone else,
Accept and forgive, learn and release,
Take charge of your life and yourself.

Always express your love,
To the person who lives in your heart,
The harm you cause by withholding your love,
May cause them to grow apart.

Share your light which glistens,
From where you've been cracked open by the pain,
Whisper from your heart to your lover,
Let flow what should not be contained.

Janine Palmer (Silver Moon)

Any hell

Rest when life gets weary,
When people are unkind, disengage,
When life is reflecting conflict,
Take the lesson then turn the page.

What does anything teach you?
Are you open to facing yourself?
Are you ready to put down your wooden cross?
And step out of any hell?

Have you learned about the aspects of yourself?
The higher and lower parts?
The one who reaches out a hand to help another,
And the one who would rather throw darts.

Do you breathe in God's love?
And do you share it with your brother?
Or do you think you're separate or superior?
Thinking your brother is the other.

In life you create your journey,
In life you guide your sail,
In life there are hills and valleys,
And upon the ocean still breezes and gales.

What do you create by your actions?
By your decisions what treasures or costs?
By your responses or your reactions,
Do you experience abundance or loss?

Some days are for singing,
Some are for work or play,
Some for crying and reflection,
And some for making a new way.

But ever are we creators,
We create here the entire time,
Do you create heaven or hell?
And is it yours or mine?

Janine Palmer (Silver Moon)

Tranquility

She never would have dreamed or imagined,
Who she discovered she was through grace,
But her guides began to show her,
Mirrored glimpses hidden there in place.

Glimpses of things about her, hidden,
To be revealed when the time was right,
It was remembering and then being humble,
That she was here to help bring in the light.

So many things are forgotten,
When we descend here through the veil,
And wisdom comes through trials and initiations,
And the shattering of locks and nails.

Some of her guides were ancestors,
Of previous incarnations here,
Others were ascended masters and star beings,
Our way for ascension they are helping to clear.

Some were angels of higher spirit,
Never having taken physical shape,
In this lower vibrational, temporary earth school,
The trip here we are so brave to make.

But most of us do not recall,
Who we really are,
Or that earth is not our true home,
We hail from the stars.

So when she began to discover,
Different parts and aspects of her being,
And after opening to trust her truth,
She was astounded with what she was seeing.

She discovered such depth of compassion,
Which needed to be balanced with logic too,
And she had to remove many ropes and cords,
To allow her power to come back through.

The love she was drew in many,
They were drawn to her to reconnect,
Sharing what she knew about Oneness,
It's fixed ideologies and judgment we must reject.

In gratitude she would pray,
And in gratitude she would live,
It didn't mean she didn't struggle,
But her calling was to heal and give.

She honored her duty as a messenger,
She worked with strength and grace,
She was a warrior in peace and tranquility,
To help remove masks to reveal the true face.

Some would resist the shadow side,
Some would stumble in fear,
Some would let go of attachment,
To rise above their trails of tears.

Some would learn to rise above,
The limitation of the ancestor's pain,
Some would ascend lifting their ancestors and brethren,
To where truth and love do reign.

Love she began to find in herself,
And then happiness began to fill her soul,
Her heart began to heal and blossom,
Beyond the illusions to where true love flows.

Janine Palmer (Spirit Silver Moon)

They Resurrect

Someone who has seen the darkness,
Can more fully appreciate the light,
Having gained seeds of wisdom's treasure,
Which glows with unknown possibilities bright.

And the things they find to heal themselves,
Many will share now with you too,
At certain times in certain circumstances,
When you're ready for it to come through.

Some people see us in mysterious ways,
They see things in us we don't see in ourselves,
Sometimes others will resurrect in us,
Things for awareness which were forgotten on shelves.

They might let loose certain monsters,
Which needed to come out,
They might cause us tears, anger or sadness,
And we might heal when we shout.

They or we might tap into something dormant,
Some hidden wisdom lying there within us,
Opening us to ancient knowing,
For ourselves now fully to trust.

They might bring to our awareness,
Something of a gift we possess,
And then we might hear the call of our soul,
To share it with the rest.

Janine Palmer (Silver Moon)

Powerful and Pure

Her presence here was compassion,
She was a messenger here to heal,
But there were those of lower vibrational frequencies,
And her energy they would try to steal.

They were in the grip of the ego,
Which likes to be the center of attention,
Wanting to be worshiped, feeding off false energy,
Which is not of higher intention.

Some people can see through other's masks,
Others follow along like sheep,
We can choose to detach or disengage from,
These beings who walk in their sleep.

But they do not only walk in their sleep,
They talk in their sleep as well,
And when they do they might keep themselves and others,
Stuck in a deep, dark well.

Only they do not see it,
They care more about themselves than others,
They are disconnected from the collective,
As evidenced by their treatment of their sisters and their brothers.

The beings of Light who guide her,
Said she was powerful and pure,
Because of the light coming through her,
Her compassion was strong and true and sure.

There are those who might not recognize,
The vibration from her that heals,
And in misunderstanding, jealousy or ignorance,
Their lower vibrational energy they and others will feel.

A mirror might be held up to them,
To reflect the energy they're putting out,
And it is up to the individual,
Whether weeds or flowers sprout.

When drama, chaos and unpleasantness,
Is staring you back in the face,
What is it trying to show you in need of healing,
To bring you back to a state of grace?

No enlightened being,
Would present falseness against another,
Because higher vibrational frequency won't sustain it,
Because we are of the One and there is no 'other'.

Some stand here in false light,
It's the ego's illusion at large,
It the negative end of the spectrum,
In need of a positive charge.

And you can choose to engage in it,
Or you can learn to detach and move on,
What you experience is what you create,
Are you your ego's pawn?

Janine Palmer (Silver Moon)

Needs Must

I must be able to look at myself,
From different perspectives to grow and learn,
I need to listen to things people say,
My own balance is an elixir I earn.

We must learn to accept our shadow side,
Even if others do not,
They are happy enough to point it out,
Just in case we forgot.

And sometimes we do forget them,
For reasons which differ for all,
There are treasures to be found in the dirt,
And we can only see them when we fall.

I know I must always be aware,
Of how what I do or say affects another,
Because it is never my aim or intention,
To offend or harm my brother.

If my brother misunderstands me,
Thinking I have committed some crime,
Which I know in truth I did not do,
How I react determines whether I fall or climb.

Sometimes other's negative energy,
Might draw us in to a terrible storm,
And we get to decide whether to remain there,
And whether it teaches us or leaves us torn.

I know I must take a step back,
To view my behavior, actions and intentions,
In order for improvement and healing that's needed,
To remove me from any stagnant suspension.

When I become aware of things about myself,
Which at first I might not like what I see,
I have to find why and where correction is needed,
Which will help me become a better version of me.

But this also includes acceptance of self,
Not feeing unworthy in any dark way,
Others will always find fault with us,
But self-love with us must always remain.

I don't have to hide my darker side,
I don't need to be ashamed,
I simply need to find the balance between the two,
In the absence of guilt or fear or blame.

Janine Palmer (Silver Moon)

Shedding Skins & Shells

hints and Clues

Life is a mysterious puzzle,
With a few hints and clues,
To discover more about who you are,
And what you create by what you choose.

There are little pointers,
People who see parts of you,
And if you are open to this knowledge,
You will blossom as light flows through.

As you work through and release the falsehoods,
The programming, misinformation and lies,
Your truth rises to the surface,
And you will shed the nefarious disguise.

That disguise does not belong to you,
It's not part of who you really are,
It was part of the test of finding your truth,
Even though hidden, your truth was never far.

The way you evolve is so beautiful,
The chrysalis ever transforms,
Out of the dark you emerge with your wings,
With new strength from weathering storms.

Janine Palmer (Silver Moon)

Bless

He said bless the things that matter,
Be in gratitude every day,
And you will carve out along your path,
A demonstration of the light and the way.

Be a wisdom keeper,
Shed the burden of lies,
Greet your inner knowing,
Step out of your disguise.

Peel off that mask you wear,
It's outdated, a cumbersome dead weight,
It's a falsehood you used to hide behind,
Before you found the gate.

Before your heart was opened,
You were led around by your mind,
Which is limited and it was programmed,
To keep you stuck in fear and spiritually blind.

There is more to your reality,
Than the things you have been taught,
There is more to your reality,
Than the falsehoods you have bought.

Some of us are modern prophets,
I am a preacher for the light,
To remind you of your beauty,
And it's not about wrong or right.

You are worthy of the highest love,
Because it is your home,
You're not a slave to the veil,
When you lift the veil, you atone.

Janine Palmer (Silver Moon)

Ghosts

Ghosts they come in many forms,
They whisper to us to learn,
They encourage us to open our eyes,
And to shed illusions to be burned.

The ghosts could be our memories,
And what we choose to hold onto,
Those debilitating perceptions we carry,
Which block us and are untrue.

They block our forward movement,
Until we release them and let them go,
Which will open us up to new blessings,
More wondrous than we know.

We cannot really move forward,
If we are clinging to a dead horse,
The ghosts whisper to us reminders,
To learn from a higher source.

The higher source is part of us,
But we forgot it when we came,
So here on earth we must rise above
This insidious, challenging little game.

We must remember our magnificence,
We must remember our divinity,
We must shed and burn the falsehoods,
Which so many falsely believe.

When we release the pain which binds us,
We take our power back,
We have all we need within us,
There is nothing which we lack.

So many people are searching,
Outside of themselves for things,
Which are safely stored inside themselves,
Of which our hearts and souls do sing.

We must open to our true selves,
By letting go of pain and lies,
Some things we believe are so untrue,
And we recognize not the disguise.

Janine Palmer (Silver Moon)

False hell

She battled through the riff raff,
She climbed the mountains tall,
She bandaged up her bruises,
Every time she took a fall.

She shared the energy of her compassion,
Which came from the deepest love divine,
She did her best from the remembered knowledge,
Trudging through the muck of the swine.

Sometimes when she would wash the filth away,
In some tranquil cleansing pond,
Her reflection was something she often didn't recognize,
Because there were times she had come undone.

Sometimes she resembled a haggard warrior,
Sometimes she was a mother of love very deep,
Sometimes she was wife and mother,
And sometimes they didn't recognize her and left her to weep.

But the strength she ever needed,
Could always be found within herself,
And in nature always replenishing,
She tore away and burned any remnants of false hell.

Janine Palmer (Silver Moon)

Broken Glass

Something called her to the woods that day,
To the place where her heart soared free,
Wondering what treasures or secrets would reveal themselves,
When we are open there is always something to see.

As she walked along the forest path,
Which her moccasined feet knew so well,
Something cracked and crunched under her feet,
And she heard the tone of a bell.

She stopped short for closer inspection,
Only to find it was broken glass very fine and thin,
She was curious as to where it had come from,
Then she glanced over and saw him grin.

She stood in surprise as he sat there,
Leaning against an old stump,
His hands were covering his glowing heart,
And she could swear she could her it thump.

She approached him knowing he needed help,
She asked, 'What has happened here?'
He said, I shattered the glass encasing my heart."
And from his eye escaped a tear.

He said, 'I knew it was time to shed my armor,
To allow my heart to be free,
But now that I have, I don't know what to do,
I'm afraid it might continue to bleed.'

She knelt before him gently lifting his hands,
To have a closer glance,
She said, 'You will need to allow it to release some things,
Let it flow dear, give it a chance.'

Upon closer inspection of his heart,
Its glow was slightly dim,
She asked him if he would like her help,
And nodded to her with a grin.

She held her hands above his heart,
Sending healing love and light,
She whispered something foreign to him,
And she blew on it as he watched it glow bright.

She said, 'You need to send love to your heart,
Love is in everything and all around,
Draw in divine love energy,
And blessings will then abound.'

She said, 'Now that you have freed your heart,
You can allow good blessings to come in,
Trust yourself and your brave decision,
And allow this new part of your journey to begin.'

He took her hands and kissed them,
He thanked her from the love in his heart,
She grinned at him eyes a twinkle,
And said, 'This is a very good start.'

Janine Palmer (Silver Moon)

Dead Wood

Do you have any dead wood attached to you?
Anything old and dead to clear?
So the rest of you that is alive and well,
Will be more open to see and hear.

The dead wood from experiences,
The dead wood from false perception,
The dead wood from old wounds,
The dead wood from fear and rejection.

The dead wood which keeps you chained,
The dead wood which so distracts you,
The dead wood which no longer serves a purpose,
The dead wood disrupting your energy from flowing through.

Sometimes we can't hear our higher voice,
Because we are too distracted by the old,
There comes a time to take control of things,
There are new experiences to have and stories to be told.

Take up a tool and get to work,
Take up a powerful tool of your choice,
And cut away any energy to the dead wood,
To free yourself and your voice.

Janine Palmer (Silver Moon)

The Trigger

The word was just a trigger,
For things to be released,
For anger, pain and sadness,
To welcome some relief.

The word was just a trigger,
The gun was already loaded,
All that she had stored inside,
For all the times she had been goaded.

For all of the harassment,
For the resistance to her love,
For all of the cruel things he ever said,
To crush the spirit of the dove.

Does he simply not recognize?
The beauty he continued to crush?
Because of fears and power and pain,
When will enough be enough?

And what if she finds the courage,
To walk away from that shell?
What if one day she goes dancing out,
Of his torment and self-created hell?

Skipping out of the hell of the past,
And into a future bright,
Into a future she creates herself,
With the brilliance of her own light.

Because she does believe in dragons,
And she knows that God is there,
Ever and always inside her,
The Source of her light so fair.

The neglect and abuse must stop one day,
When people see the light,
When they have had enough of the effects,
When others don't treat them right.

Mistreatment comes from a place of pain,
A hellish pain so deep,
That the person who wallows in it,
It in a self-induced and armored sleep.

Feel free to detach from the pain,
When you know it does not serve,
And reconnect to the brilliant blessing,
Which is your radiant verve.

Janine Palmer (Silver Moon)

Powerful Potion

Do you feel it move within you?
Can you feel it swirling around?
Do you know what I am talking about?
Where can your love be found?

There is so much within you,
But maybe you forgot,
Because of how life gets in the way,
The haves and the have nots.

The trick is not to identify,
With every thought which does come in,
Because so many are untrue,
And so the struggle begins.

There is love within you,
There is love from friends all around,
There is love all around you in energy,
And from the Divine it can ever be found.

Sometimes we must be cracked open,
For the love and light to get in,
To release the pain we carry,
To disconnect from the falsehood of sin.

We hold so much against ourselves,
Due false beliefs about 'sin',
And when we rise above the programming,
Our true healing can begin.

Because you are a being of immense love,
You are here to learn and grow,
And when you open your heart to it,
Endless love will begin to flow.

Janine Palmer (Silver Moon)

Your Demon

What is your demon trying to tell you?
What challenging things continue to present?
And what are you supposed to learn from them?
And then move on and not lament.

It isn't even really 'your' demon,
But maybe a fear you have not faced,
A battle you have not conquered,
Only a step away from grace.

It is really only a teacher,
A drill sergeant in your mind,
To train you and test you to rise above,
While in this training ground of time.

Are you aware of the illusions all around you?
Are you aware of the things you have drawn in?
Are you aware you create your own reality?
Your own heaven or hell with no sin.

So the demon is there for a reason,
And you are in charge of when it goes,
But your lower self doesn't know this,
Only your higher self really knows.

But it takes courage and awareness,
To step out of your lower self,
When your shell is well cracked open,
And you can walk right out of your hell.

It's only an illusion anyway,
Conjured up by fear,
When you give away your power,
Because your vision is unclear.

When you awaken to your inner truth,
And your outer shell is cracked open wide,
When your vision clears and sharpens,
Behind your masks you will no longer hide.

Janine Palmer (Silver Moon)

Bloody Armor

Will you put down your bloody armor?
The vehicle which carries your wounds unhealed;
They don't see the healing light of day,
Keeping yourself numb so you don't heal.

The blood all over your armor,
Is no one else's but your own,
For any perceived regrets or mistakes,
By your own forgiveness you will atone.

If you knew you could feel better,
Would you release your hold on your pain?
Would you release it to higher dimensions to be healed?
And open to what you could gain?

Would you continue clearing out the old,
To make room for blessings anew?
Would you take a look at the closed door of forgiveness,
To see what treasures are there for you?

Would you stop holding so many things against yourself?
Against your beloved Sacred Heart?
Would you bathe in the cool refreshing, healing waters,
Of your inner kingdom where all truth starts?

Would you wash away the old pain?
Like dust and grime off of your skin?
With the cleansing antidote of your own forgiveness,
For your new life now to begin.

Would you listen to the angels,
Who you can't see all around you and up above?
Their whispers of deep devotion to you,
To reconnect you with your love.

Life is about the warriors.
What they learn and how they grow,
How they rise above their own ashes,
Remembering their divinity and rekindling their glow.

Janine Palmer (Silver Moon)

Resentment

Why do we hold resentment?
Against others, a festering stew,
Which is a toxic poison to the vessel which holds it,
Preventing new blessings from coming through.

Why do we keep ourselves in prison,
To the resentment we feel and hold?
Why do we allow our energy,
To be used or bought or sold?

Resentment is a prison,
Limiting like a ball and chain,
Holding us back from new experiences,
And the blessings we would gain.

What if we released that resentment?
Peel it off and release it right now,
Give it to the light or the angels,
To begin the healing you deserve somehow.

Stop holding things against others,
Stop holding things against yourself,
And you will release yourself from that prison,
And you will walk right out of hell.

Janine Palmer (Silver Moon)

Initiations & Battle Scars

Traps

On this gauntlet of a journey,
This initiation of shadow and light,
You shall be tested to discover your mettle,
And your inner warrior might.

There are stealthy things and booby traps,
And land mines along your way,
You must remain aware and learn to bend,
With the branches as they sway.

There is programming on this planet,
In which man is often ensnared,
The trick is to carve your own path through the mists,
As many before you have dared.

Surround yourself with your heavenly light,
Your armor you can barely see,
And know that the protection and support you need,
Can always be found within thee.

This Mystery School of Life,
Of which many are unaware,
Will test you but will also guide you,
It's a challenge which we all share.

We can endeavor to support each other,
With honor and best intentions,
Or we can judge, shun and ignore,
Which will require our higher Self's intervention.

Part of the journey is getting in touch,
With your intuitive higher Self,
And being aware that the ego serves us,
But should not control us, as that is hell.

The higher self is connected to heaven,
To our beloved Source,
The lower self, our insidious ego,
Is the darker devil of course.

Janine Palmer (Silver Moon)

Treasure Beneath

Behind every scar is a story, of something which helped you learn,
We are forged in the fires of life, only when we burn;
Some things happen for reasons, which at first may be unknown,
But we soon see how they teach us, as deeper things are shown.

Things which create scars redirect us, along our wandering path,
There is beauty when we find the good, creating ripple effects which last,
Everything has a ripple effect, do you watch your ripples grow?
They expand in good or bad ways, which you might not even know.

What story does your scar tell?
Does it speak of heaven or does it speak of hell?
What if you changed your perspective, what if it was like a tattoo?
What if it represented, a stronger version of you?

What if you look beyond the scar, yours or someone else's?
To the warrior who survived and the knowledge they now share?
How did it forge them and shape them, in their personal, silent fire?
How did they learn to rise above the pain, or in it are they still mired?

Listen to the story of someone's scar, they heal as the story is told,
It's when we let go of something, that it no longer has a hold,
When we determine to let go of pain and release it to the light,
We give up our inner battles and we no longer have to fight.

Look at the scars as reminders, of the beauty found within,
Remember they are outward reminders, to disconnect from inner sin;
Sin is a misconceived notion, it means we have missed the mark,
When we recognize our own magnificence, we rise above out of the dark.

Scars are a thing of beauty and if someone cannot see past,
Then they haven't yet found the truth within, they struggle through earth school's path;
When we look past the superficial, to the treasure buried deep,
We wake up from our collective coma and no longer do we sleep.

Janine Palmer (Silver Moon)

Elixir or Poison?

Is it a door or is it a window?
Is it a pinpoint of light or a maze?
Do you wave your hand blindly in front of yourself?
Trying to see through the haze?

Where is the switch to your inner light?
Inside you it glows and burns;
Find the switch of your divinity,
Flip it and another page you will turn.

How do we turn the pages,
Of the book of our lives, my friends?
Who is writing our stories?
It's us with the help the Creator lends.

The Creator sends us people,
They are teachers as we go,
To help us learn from experiences,
And to help us evolve and grow.

When we rise above life's obstacles,
It is then that we turn the page,
But we cannot move forward if we don't rise above,
We can't move forward in guilt or shame or rage.

But another way to flip the switch,
Another way to turn the page,
Is to forgive yourself and others,
And from negativity to disengage.

You create your own reality,
With the thoughts you continually think,
You have to consume what you offer yourself,
Is it elixir or poison you drink?

Janine Palmer (Silver Moon)

Above & Beyond

Through these initiations,
We rise ever above and beyond,
We learn to release and detach from,
Things we are not very fond.

To release what no longer serves us,
To take back the power that is ours,
To break free of our self-made prisons,
To tend to and heal our scars.

Our scars are potent reminders,
Of things we have bravely survived,
They remind us of our courage,
How we have overcome and thrived.

Above and beyond is Ascension,
It's a type of Self rebirth,
It's rising out of the ashes,
It's reconnecting with our verve.

We are radiant beings,
We come from love and light,
We are here to remember or worth,
And to shine our light so bright.

We are divine co-creators,
With a God we cannot describe,
A God whose energy is pure love,
We are One Divine Soul Tribe.

Janine Palmer (Silver Moon)

Battles

Everyone battles something,
There are demons at the door,
Battles won and battles lost,
And lessons by the score.

But every battle creates the warrior,
Every battle evolves the soul,
And the more we rise above the battles,
The brighter our soul light glows,

What do you weave into your braid?
What experiences are woven in there?
What teachings from your ancestors,
Add to your personal flair?

What do you hide in your witch's hat?
What healing knowledge do you carry?
That was ever and always for the good,
And was never anything scary.

For millennia people's misperceptions
Have knocked man off his course,
And from the divine light of creator,
They have somehow become divorced.

They have wandered so far from divine light,
They have forgotten just who they are,
They stumble over the roots of the tree of life,
Not really knowing where they are.

How can their tree of life,
Prosper and grow in neglect,
When they cut the roots which feed it,
As illusions, fear and shame attest.

We do not nurture our beautiful souls,
With the falsehoods and lies here on earth,
The truth comes from our own spirit,
Our Creator put it there first.

It is only when we lay down,
At the roots of the tree of life,
The weapons and armor we carry,
Our battles and wounds and strife.

Janine Palmer (Silver Moon)

Triggered Memories

Memories remind us of experiences,
Whether they are good or bad,
They remind us of things which shaped us or taught us,
We get to choose whether to be happy or sad.

Certain things will trigger,
Thoughts of things now past,
And sometimes certain patterns,
Create suffering which too long lasts.

We needn't really suffer so long,
If we can learn how to detach,
Even if only to a small degree,
To open a new door's waiting latch.

Will your memory be a guide?
Or will it be a trigger and turn on old pain?
To engage an outdated program,
Which does not serve you once again.

The memories can be a reminder,
Of how you have evolved,
Of something that shaped your growth,
And not some problem to be solved.

Remember forgiveness and release,
Are a remedy of great proportion,
Of how you have risen above and beyond,
Don't allow it to be a distortion.

Perspectives have a huge effect,
On the way we think we feel,
If we can change our perspective now and again,
That will help to keep it real.

Janine Palmer (Silver Moon)

Spirit Guide

The being was a guide who had mastered,
Lessons in the physical realm,
Rising above ego and back to spirit,
Now the master of his own helm.

The being was an ascended guide,
To watch over an initiate here,
To guide with spiritual whispers,
If the initiate would be open to hear.

He watched her engage in a relationship,
One to which she had felt called,
He watched over the years as she struggled,
To break through his fortress walls.

The guide watched the kindhearted woman,
Give all of her heart and soul to a man,
But he appeared not to see it or honor it,
And there's only so long and un-watered flower can stand.

She gave to him as long as she could,
But due to his fears and old pain he couldn't fully give back,
So the void which was created grew and grew,
Manifesting into starvation from lack.

When there is such an imbalance,
The giver will cease to give,
Because they are not adequately nurtured or fed,
And so they search for new reasons to live.

But that is not the saddest part,
In vain she would always try to communicate,
But he wouldn't hear what she spoke from her soul,
He perceived it as some kind of hate.

When she would cry from a place like a gutter,
He'd leave her lying there with no help,
He would throw her words back at her there,
Only focused upon himself.

He couldn't be bothered to extend a hand,
To lift her out of that place,
Where he had forced her and left her heart to bleed,
And himself he could never face.

The guide could see their journey was through,
And he sent new friends along her path,
They saw the beauty of her heart and soul,
And with their help she slowly took her life back.

They reflected her goodness back to her,
They nurtured her soul which was starved,
They were welcomed by her into her heart,
And their names there were happily carved.

Janine Palmer (Silver Moon)

Kinks

There are kinks in life which block the flow,
Of the life force energy and healing our verve,
There are people, places and situations,
Which trigger, nurture or harm our nerve.

Things present along our paths,
As teachers and tests to strengthen our mettle,
To teach us to be aware where we walk,
Is it flowers and grass or weeds and nettles?

People's actions may feel harmful,
But we might not see the pain behind it, their cost,
We might think only of our 'little' self,
And so an important lesson might be lost.

Man-made religions may ease a kink or create one,
It all depends upon the higher plan,
And what is meant to be learned or conquered,
Depending on the choices and actions of the (wo)man.

How do we learn to process and release,
Any thoughts or feelings about things?
Do our emotions teach us or keep us prisoner?
Do we open or close to the blessings life brings?

We might not even recognize the blessings,
If we are in a defensive position trying to prove we are right,
And in staying in a lower vibrational energy,
We might introduce our self to the soul's dark night.

No one can fix anything for us,
Unless we open up enough and ask,
Unless we allow the spiritual healing,
When we've learned from the looking glass.

Teachers are not always people,
They might be animals, places or things,
Situations called in to test you,
On higher levels for the strength they bring.

If you break down and crumble to your knees,
Don't despair there's something for you down there,
You will find it on the other side of acceptance and surrender,
And forgiveness is the freshest breath of healing air.

You will create kinks in life and learn to release them,
If you don't, your energy won't flow,
And the build-up of pressure within you,
Will build and build until it blows.

How did or do the kinks of life redirect you?
What patience and strength did you acquire?
Did you learn to be more open to things?
To be at peace and embrace what transpires.

Janine Palmer (Silver Moon)

Bygones

He said to me bygones are bygones,
Because he knew the way I'd been hurt,
It's good advice and it's wisdom's truth,
When we learn from being on our knees in the dirt.

When beings come to a separation of paths,
From pain created by things known and unknown,
When they discover they are on different levels,
When they evolve from the experiences they are shown.

Some of us stay stuck in pain,
And from that pain we might harm our brother,
Unless and until we learn to release the pain,
Then painful lessons we will continue to discover.

We might just push good people away,
Standing stubbornly in our position of being right,
Thinking we are justified but we all learn,
From the darkness and/or the light.

So when we can forgive and move forward,
When we can let go and then walk away,
When we can let bygones now be bygones,
We raise our vibration every day.

It doesn't mean it didn't hurt,
The way someone hurled the venom of their pain toward us,
But it means we love ourselves enough,
To disconnect from another's dogmatic rust.

We learned from their behavior,
As we learn from our behavior too,
How it guides, reflects or redirects us,
To open us to allow our love to flow through.

We might not be able to continue to interact,
With someone who thinks they are holier than thou,
While they fling their poison arrows in judgment,
But we can still let bygones be bygones now.

Because of our higher vibration,
Because we have learned to forgive and not stay stuck,
Because we have learned to take responsibility for our actions,
And not pass the righteousness buck.

So yes let bygones be bygones,
Even if it means saying goodbye,
To the life you knew once upon a time,
Or a once trusted friend who pulled a knife.

Take that knife from the sleepwalker,
And use it to cut the cords,
Which will allow any negativity to keep running through,
When they are not open to love or the word.

Thank you Bryan

Janine Palmer (Silver Moon)

Tribes

To raise a hand against another,
For reasons of pain, control or power,
Is to damage part of your higher self,
To piss of your own inner flower.

What energy you put out into the world.
Affects the collective vibe,
You create karma which must be balanced with love,
Through your interaction with different tribes.

To hold anything against yourself,
To hold anything against a brother,
Is to affect your very own life force,
And your own spirit do you smother.

When the pain you carry,
Comes out in nasty ways,
It is a very clear reflection,
That you can't see through the haze.

Any ignorant and embarrassing behavior,
Is your old pain coming forth,
Misdirected and if intended to harm,
Steers you backwards on your course.

What you do not overcome,
What you might fail to rise above,
Will keep you coming back until you learn the lesson,
Which is not to push and shove.

When we choose not to dwell in unforgiveness,
Is when we choose to take our power back,
When we choose to rebirth ourselves from the ashes,
We find there is nothing that we lack.

But in order to learn of ascension,
We must first be pushed to our knees,
And when we stop fighting and lashing out,
We find new blessings will flow free.

When we come to a place of acceptance,
That is when things begin to flow,
Surrender is a type of gate,
Directing you to blessings unknown.

Humility is divine strength,
Silence is a quiet tool,
To propel you out of the pit of hell,
Into a wise being instead of a fool.

Janine Palmer (Silver Moon)

Judgment & Ego

Ego Burns Our Wings

So often we seem to stumble though life,
Getting hammered and carrying pain,
Then trying to move forward in a positive way,
And sometimes that endeavor's in vain.

A man once told me a story,
He spoke of the high and the low,
He told me of different parts of myself,
I previously did not know.

He said I have a lower self,
Which comes from judgment and fear,
And he said I have a higher self,
Which comes from love and cheer.

The higher Self is connected,
To Source, The All, The One,
The lower self is connected to ego,
Which judges and it shuns.

The ego is here to test us,
It tries to protect us and keep us safe,
It doesn't recognize the higher part of us,
Which is our Light and Truth and Grace.

The ego thinks we are separate,
From our brother man,
It forgot we are all connected,
To One Source, One Tribe, One Clan.

So when we finally awaken,
To our connectedness to the All,
That is when we begin to repair,
The damage from the fall.

We are here to rise above,
Lower vibrations resembling hell,
To the light of our true home,
Where our spirit dwells.

When we learn awareness,
Of the ego, which tests us here,
And we learn to rise above it,
That it rising to love from fear.

What he spoke of was Ascension,
Rising above falsehoods and lies,
That we are regaining our sacred wings,
And remembering how to fly.

We are remembering our magnificence,
We are remembering our origins divine,
We are remembering to love our brother,
Because we are connected to the same vine.

But if we are not careful,
The ego will burn our wings,
If we don't take our power back,
We'll have no voice with which to sing.

Janine Palmer (Silver Moon)

Fly

Is it my imagination?
Is it only a dream?
These other-dimensional experiences…
Are they more than what they seem?

What are these wings they show me?
Which I often wear?
To do my higher work?
For my brethren over there?

When I become aware of ego,
And when I detach from that,
I rise out of that hellfire,
To where enlightenment is at.

And when I choose to disengage,
From the illusions, drama and lies,
I can fly through higher dimensions,
And see with my soul's eyes.

I can see the beauty of everything,
I can feel the love all around,
It carries me and supports me,
It connects me to what keeps me sound.

The whispers of the Holy Spirit,
Which guides me on my wings,
Is the heavenly angel's music,
Which to my heart does sing.

Janine Palmer (Silver Moon)

Side Show

A side show is not the main event,
It serves a lesser purpose in the scheme of things,
Just like with ego and the higher self,
One is a servant and one is king.

The higher self is connected to Source,
The higher self is connected to soul,
The lower self is the ego,
The servant which tries to steal the glow.

The ego is just a side show,
Which is always grasping for control,
It keeps us stuck in fear and illusion,
Which makes it hard to evolve and grow.

Allow the ego to serve you,
But don't get caught up in its snare;
Take a step back and be a witness to its antics,
But let it not interfere with your higher lair.

Be aware of the mists all around you,
Be aware of illusion's false trap,
And how it might fool you and distract you from,
Your true course and finding your map.

Walk your journey in beauty,
In confidence rise above fear,
Remember your magnificence and divinity,
When the veil is lifted, all will be clear.

Janine Palmer (Silver Moon)

The Warrior's Field

The shaman was teaching his students,
Ancient wisdom did he share,
For truth and higher purpose,
For rising above the ego's liar.

He said, This earth is the warrior's field,
It holds pain and it holds riches,
But so many beings existing here,
Have become their ego's bitches.

They are fully in the talon's grip,
Of their ego and lower vibration,
While beating their chests saying they are doing god's work,
It's really an abomination.

But the law of karma is always at play,
And many are stuck in karmic loops,
They continually jump through hoops of fire,
Trying to fit in with trifling egoic groups.

Their egos always want to be right,
Their egos love to be so offended,
Trying so desperately to strengthen their sense of self,
And so the cycles goes on and on un-ended.

Until the day comes when they pull their heads out,
Of that dark and retentive abyss,
When on their knees they re-open to their divinity,
In acceptance and surrender they receive the angel's kiss.

When they accept the darkness they've created,
By their choices and actions they made,
When they surrender any attachment to it to the light,
They enter through blessings' new gate.

And so when a brother or sister,
Will honor each being along their path,
Then the hard knocks of the warrior's field,
Will stop kicking them in the ass.

And so the shaman did chuckle,
Because humor is ever a part,
Of this and other dimensions,
And we should laugh at ourselves for a start.

We should try not to take things too seriously,
But always beware the way we treat our brothers,
Creates the reality here we will face,
We must not separate ourselves from the others.

Peace.

Janine Palmer (Silver Moon)

The Alpha Male & Female

She had to learn to be strong,
With all the men she encountered in her life,
Strong like a warrior with a shield of love,
To withstand their ego, or victim, or pain or strife.

Because she too was an Alpha,
The other half of the strength,
But because of the field of his ego which precedes him,
He usually couldn't see past his own length.

Some of them could see her,
Some had risen above,
Some knew how to honor her,
Some knew the power of love.

Some were caught up in their egos,
Pounding their so-called Alpha chests,
But the reality was until they recognized her Alpha strength,
They missed the point and fruit of the test.

Some would walk all over their women,
They would bruise them and crush them full score,
And they constantly run into the walls they create,
It's about the balance needed, then, now and forevermore.

But because of that raging ego,
Or that victim mentality and rage,
Some don't see the love and compassion,
Which is written delicately across life's pages.

The love and compassion of the Alpha female,
Her quiet but radiant power,
And when she is recognized and nurtured,
She will blossom like the most beautiful flower.

She is meant to balance him,
To compliment, nurture and share,
But when he's too busy trying to control and demean,
He invites her wrath and/or karma so fair.

Kudos to the man who is strong enough,
To love his woman divine,
To recognize how she balances him,
Who needs not depend on the ego, the drug, or the wine.

He who puts nothing before her,
Especially ego's dark thief,
He who recognizes that the ego,
Is neither master, nor warrior, nor chief.

The ego only serves to test us,
The ego wears a mask of bluster,
The ego should not be our master,
Or our life will lose its luster.

Don't buy into the darkness,
Of the illusion or the need for control,
Because if you do you are nothing but a pawn,
Who has lost sight of thy true holy goal.

Hail the balanced Alpha,
The masculine and feminine halves of the whole,
The overcoming and rising above lower illusions here,
To re-establish the balance, as above so below.

Janine Palmer (Silver Moon)

The Deceiver

The deceiver is our ego,
Which serves us to a degree,
The deceiver is the darkness in us and all around us,
The truth is we are free.

The story is being written,
Every day you live your life,
The key is to cut the cords,
With what doesn't serve you with your knife.

To depart from negative energies,
To balance karma with great love,
To listen to the whispers now,
From the wisdom of the dove.

To rise above ego and to listen,
To the wisdom of your spirit now,
To tap into the wisdom of your higher self,
Your heart will show you how.

To honor all beings with love and respect,
Which you would hope to receive,
Release and rise above any outdated falsehoods,
To which your ego cleaves.

Because the ego is only a servant,
It is not your god or boss,
But only when you elevate your thinking,
Above the limitations of old dross.

Tell the deceiver, no thank you,
Tell the deceiver your will,
Tell the deceiver to run along now,
Because you want no part of its hell.

Janine Palmer (Silver Moon)

The Suffering & Shadow

Shadows

Sometimes the shadows beckon,
And maybe time is needed there,
But things don't blossom in the dark,
So for balance we must have a care.

There is evolving in the darkness,
It directs us toward the light,
It teaches us valuable lessons,
Of when to surrender and when to fight.

Don't flee into the shadows,
Don't get drawn into the fear,
Don't listen to those false thoughts,
Which cause many unnecessary tears.

Take the time you need for reflection,
Take the time you need for release,
Be in charge of your own light,
Don't let darkness be a thief.

Open the door to your waiting heart,
Find the wisdom there inside,
Open your soul to connect with it,
In the shadows you no longer abide.

Janine Palmer (Silver Moon)

Just Doing a Dance

So many of us are just doing a dance,
We're not ready to let go of the pain,
If we continue to feed it and live there,
In our very own personal hell and wonder what we'll gain.

Our soul will gain evolvement,
When we finally agree,
That is time to take our power back,
And open our spiritual eyes to see,

When we begin to recognize,
That hell is not our home,
We will rise above the illusion,
And no longer will we roam.

We roam in search of answers,
We think they're outside of ourselves,
It's only when we find our truth within,
That we can step out of that hell.

Are you doing a dance with darkness?
Are you under darkness's spell?
Can you see the pinpoint of light within you,
Directing you out of hell?

Only you can do it,
You don't do it by existing in hate,
You don't do it by attacking your brother,
That's not the way to the gate.

Find your truth my brother,
Use your free will choice,
Don't endeavor to take up outdated causes,
Be a warrior not for darkness's voice.

Janine Palmer (Silver Moon)

Broken Sword

In the woods while she was walking,
One day in the hollow of a tree,
She found an old sword hidden there,
And so she pulled it free.

A jolt of electric current,
Seemed to radiate through her being,
She looked at the reflection of the blade,
And couldn't believe what she was seeing.

A story began to unfold before her,
Being played out upon the blade,
About the experiences of an old warrior,
And the choices he had made.

He started out as a valiant knight,
He was a force mighty and fierce,
But by the end of his journey,
He was reduced to so many tears.

At first he honored all to him,
Kingdom, Lord and Liege,
Until so many battles wore him down,
A victim of the siege.

But the siege she saw wasn't just the battles,
Not just the physical fights,
It was the pain and anger he carried,
Which destroyed his verve and light.

He turned to the drink to numb his pain,
He succumbed because he could not reason,
He was taken over by thoughts unreleased,
And now ruled by demon seamen.

The demons were his anger,
The demons were his rage,
The demons were unforgiveness,
And he couldn't turn the page.

He destroyed his life with his lady,
Her life was shattered as well,
Because she loved him so,
And he drew her into his hell.

He didn't know how to let it go,
He lacked acceptance and surrender too,
The ingredients for rising above,
Which is only discovered by the few.

When he left this earthly world,
He was shown what his spirit had learned,
Through his enlightening life review,
Which he would bring with him when he returned.

He experienced some healing there,
But would bring the wisdom from his experience back,
His spirit would use that knowledge,
To help others in such lack.

He was shown the angels are with us,
And we can call upon them to assist,
That we create our reality with our thoughts,
And we can change it if we wish.

The angels are happy to help us,
We can ask by prayer, by whisper or voice,
But they cannot help until we ask,
Because of our free will choice.

He imbued the story of his experiences,
There in that broken blade,
The end was broken off in the ground,
Where his body was laid.

His loving wife then took his sword,
And placed it in the tree,
Asking for the healing forces of nature,
To set his tormented soul free.

Then she who had found the sword,
Looked closely and noticed at the end,
The sword was indeed broken there,
But she knew his heart did mend.

She gently replaced the broken sword,
Back inside the hollow of the tree,
For the next person to happen along,
And the message they would receive.

Janine Palmer (Silver Moon)

Place of Pain

She wondered about the reasons for suffering,
She pondered the results of emotional pain,
For what a being learned from the experience,
And the wisdom one then gained.

And how those feelings drive us,
Or how we try to block them out.
How we heal on our knees in surrender,
Or behind our walls we cry and shout.

She wondered if it was necessary
That in order for her to write,
That she had to be in a place of pain,
To tap into the feelings to express them just right.

The pain is the catalyst for the healing,
Writing the words serves a healing goal,
Can someone write things as beautifully,
When it's not pouring right out of their soul?

Yes they can write from memory,
They can write from experiences too,
They can tap into the feelings of the good or bad,
And allow the stories to then pour through.

So maybe it's not necessary to be in that place,
Of pain we were once in before,
But we have to have had those experiences,
To learn from them to access what's behind so many doors.

The pain is only a teacher,
In life painful things re-direct,
They direct us to other people and blessings,
And they force us to disconnect from strife and neglect.

Janine Palmer (Silver Moon)

Layers of Loss and Rust

The hinges on the door of his heart,
Were layered in loss and rust,
He'd closed the door tightly for protection,
Too leery now to open to trust.

He left behind everything familiar,
Except for his beloved little cats,
And he ventured to a new place,
To recover and learn to detach.

A repairing of his soul,
Was in process, all the times he cried,
And his path led to him good people,
Sent to him by his guides.

So he decided to open up a bit,
To allow some new friendship in,
And a curious thing happened then,
His life then began again.

Because the connections we experience in life,
Help our energy to flow,
They teach us and they guide us,
To open to remember what we know.

Hopefully soon we learn,
That to stay stagnant in anything serves us not,
When lower vibrational things we discover,
Are something we subscribe to and we bought.

He learned we have to detach to find peace,
He learned there are parts of people we will never lose,
And how we decide to look at it,
Is a perception we get to choose.

We get to decide when we are ready,
To let go of and release old pain,
And only when we do so,
Will we find what there is to gain.

There is no need to punish ourselves,
Life's experiences are quite enough,
In this reality of duality,
There is smooth and there is rough.

To learn to flow is part of it,
To learn to let go is key,
Because attachment causes suffering,
Which is a trap for you and me.

So he learned to let go of the feeling of loss,
To a very large degree,
And he blew the rust off those hinges,
Now his heart and soul can breathe.

Janine Palmer (Silver Moon)

A Reflection of Truth

She saw a glimmer of reflection,
Of her truth in someone else,
But she shunned it and rejected it,
And placed it upon a shelf.

The shelf is a place of darkness,
Where we bury things deep inside,
When we don't face the shadows and demons,
We bury them in us where they reside.

Only when we are humble,
Only when we are on our knees,
Only when we are ready to let go,
Will we face and conquer these.

Only when we forgive ourselves,
Can we then forgive others too,
Only when we remember our worth,
Will we lift the veil and rise anew.

Search for the love which is waiting there,
Discover the love which exists inside you,
Let it wash away the fears and lies,
To reveal what is real and true.

Janine Palmer (Silver Moon)

Broken Sword

In the woods while she was walking,
One day in the hollow of a tree,
She found an old sword hidden there,
And so she pulled it free.

A jolt of electric current,
Seemed to radiate through her being,
She looked at the reflection of the blade,
And couldn't believe what she was seeing.

A story began to unfold before her,
Being played out upon the blade,
About the experiences of an old warrior,
And the choices he had made.

He started out as a valiant knight,
He was a force mighty and fierce,
But by the end of his journey,
He was reduced to so many tears.

At first he honored all to him,
Kingdom, Lord and Liege,
Until so many battles wore him down,
A victim of the siege.

But the siege she saw wasn't just the battles,
Not just the physical fights,
It was the pain and anger he carried,
Which destroyed his verve and light.

He turned to the drink to numb his pain,
He succumbed because he could not reason,
He was taken over by thoughts unreleased,
And now ruled by demon seamen.

The demons were his anger,
The demons were his rage,
The demons were unforgiveness,
And he couldn't turn the page.

He destroyed his life with his lady,
Her life was shattered as well,
Because she loved him so,
And he drew her into his hell.

He didn't know how to let it go,
He lacked acceptance and surrender too,
The ingredients for rising above,
Which is only discovered by the few.

When he left this earthly world,
He was shown what his spirit had learned,
Through his enlightening life review,
Which he would bring with him when he returned.

He experienced some healing there,
But would bring the wisdom from his experience back,
His spirit would use that knowledge,
To help others in such lack.

He was shown the angels are with us,
And we can call upon them to assist,
That we create our reality with our thoughts,
And we can change it if we wish.

The angels are happy to help us,
We can ask by prayer, by whisper or voice,
But they cannot help until we ask,
Because of our free will choice.

He imbued the story of his experiences,
There in that broken blade,
The end was broken off in the ground,
Where his body was laid.

His loving wife then took his sword,
And placed it in the tree,
Asking for the healing forces of nature,
To set his tormented soul free.

Then she who had found the sword,
Looked closely and noticed at the end,
The sword was indeed broken there,
But she knew his heart did mend.

She gently replaced the broken sword,
Back inside the hollow of the tree,
For the next person to happen along,
And the message they would receive.

Janine Palmer (Silver Moon)

The Dark Tent

When she spoke of initiations,
He didn't quite know what she meant,
Stuck as he was in defense mode,
In the dark confines of his tent.

From the darkness of his perceived suffering,
He would peer out once in a while,
But it became a very lonely dungeon,
Where he lacked the urge to smile.

The tent was a place of perceived protection,
Of his thoughts and ideas of things,
His pain and memories had a special place,
In his tent where no longer did he sing.

The tent can be likened to a veil,
Something we hide or are stuck behind,
It becomes something familiar we don't want to venture from,
Which can keep us partially spiritually blind.

We cannot see as clearly through a veil,
We can't experience life fully from a tent,
We don't have to protect the remnants of painful experience,
We must process, release and vent.

Others were singing in the distance,
He could hear them in the woods through the trees,
But he was afraid to leave his dark tent unattended,
For fear someone might free his swarm of dark bees.

The bees were a buzzing distraction,
They stung him from time to time,
Did he keep them around for self-punishment?
Would he ever be able to release them from his mind?

Even though they created noise and pain,
He thought he had to protect himself and them.
So he hid inside that stagnant tent in the dark,
While the world outside let the sunshine in.

Janine Palmer (Silver Moon)

Unbending

He seemed to be so unbending,
He seemed so harsh in his wrath,
But that was just the face he presented to the world,
He kept people away by wearing a mask.

Maybe the dragon ink on his arm seemed like a warning,
But it was really love the dragon represented,
He was just selective who he shared it with,
Because of life his armor was crushed and dented.

He would rather not deal with most people,
Because what he had seen of most,
Was the shell of what they could have been,
What he saw now were shallow ghosts.

He saw traces of what they used to be,
Before life had beat them down,
But they had turned into selfish, backstabbing bastards,
And he simply wouldn't have them around.

They had harmed him and abused him,
Too many times now to tell,
And he had had enough of their tricks and lies,
And in their filth he refused to dwell.

Hardened to such a point now it seemed,
That he might just wander the road alone,
Because he had lost the ability to trust,
And there was no way to atone.

There was the rare occasion, however,
That he would cross paths with someone true,
Once in a while he would discover one of pure heart,
And he would allow that friend a tiny view.

He would interact with a select few,
He would honor them as long as they honored him,
Those who operated in integrity,
And that is when the truth of life would win.

That was when a connectedness was worthwhile,
That was when a connection would be honored in kind,
These are the little glimpses of connectedness,
One of the rare times he would allow happiness to grow on the vine.

And it was these small moments here,
In between the chaos of this hell,
That these rare friends would help heal him by small degrees,
And by small degrees parts of him would begin to feel well.

Janine Palmer (Silver Moon)

The Suffering

He was a watcher overlooking,
For a being here he was a guide,
Part of his purpose on this level,
Was to help them detach from or face what they hide.

He watched over a very kind-hearted soul,
A man of compassion who was so stuck in fear,
Fear carried over from lifetimes,
So he built walls not letting things in too near.

He would not express his feelings,
He would not listen to unfamiliar things,
He continued to struggle and suffer,
He couldn't hear his own soul's silent screams.

His conscious mind put up armor,
His conscious mind would resist,
He blocked his own forward movement,
And he resisted his lover's bold kiss.

Too fearful to allow anyone in too close,
Too fearful to open his heart,
Afraid of what might come out or in,
So his true journey he could not begin to start.

The angels sent beings along his path,
But he only recognized them to a degree,
A prisoner of his own making,
Because we wouldn't open his to his spirit to see.

He felt like a victim of everything,
Constantly giving his power away,
Not remembering or realizing the truth,
That he had the power to seize the day.

The angel whispered to him to allow the healing,
Which his body, mind and soul did so need,
But he couldn't hear through the alcoholic haze,
And his higher self's voice he continually did not heed.

If he could see past the bottom of the bottle or can,
If he would open that unknown door,
He would be shown places of familiar beauty,
Glimpses of the future, now and before.

The angel so wanted to tell him,
The fears he carries are not real,
And healing will come when he opens up,
To his heart and soul to feel.

The healing will come from detachment,
From ideas and thoughts about things,
And giving up the erroneous notion,
Of being a victim in this life stream.

The farthest energy from love is victimhood,
Victimhood is a foul prison cell,
The angel wants to tell him,
He is the key to walk out of his hell.

The angel wants to say to him,
Imagine the most beautiful feeling of love experienced here,
And that is just a fractal glimpse,
Of somethings far grander, not from here but ever so near.

That love is where we come from,
That love is where we return to,
When we step out of dogmatic illusion,
And allow our magnificent truth to shine through.

Janine Palmer (Silver Moon)

The Grief

Let us take a moment to consider,
The purpose of any grief,
To process and release our feelings which need to flow,
So they do not become a thief.

Our feelings need to be able to flow,
Like the waves of so many oceans,
They should not get stuck and fester anywhere,
Getting mixed up with untrue thoughts and emotions.

To process things we have experienced,
To process things we have learned,
To release things to the light to heal,
Because rebirth comes from things burned.

If the grief is allowed to remain,
For too long a time unreleased,
It can create dysfunction and un-wellness,
And can cause our loved ones in other dimensions unnecessary sadness and grief.

Our loved ones who have gone on before us,
Back home to a place of great love,
Don't want us to suffer due to illusions we don't understand,
And these are their whispers floating down from above.

Above is a higher dimension,
Which we have all known before,
We simply don't remember it,
When we come here through the veil of earth's door.

Talk to your loved ones now,
Out loud or in thought alone,
They hear you and know the thoughts and pain you carry,
And for them you don't need to atone.

They spirits of our loved ones are still with us,
On levels most of us can't comprehend,
They don't want us carrying guilt or prolonged grief,
And they want us to know nothing was left unsaid.

Allow them to be with you and to guide you,
And this happens when you release old grief,
So then they can more easily get through to you,
When that barrier is no longer there like a thief.

We are here to rise above,
In so many ways you know,
To rise above pain and suffering,
To new doors waiting to be shown.

Don't stare too long at any closed door,
Look through the mists of things unknown,
Be in gratitude for blessings given,
And new doors and blessings will be abundantly shown.

Janine Palmer (Silver Moon)

Illusion and the Veil

Death or Release

When a soul has completed its journey,
And it's time to go back home,
The thoughts of loved ones staying a little longer,
In earth school tend to roam.

Sometimes the learning experience here,
Feels like suffering we can no longer stand,
So when it's time to break away,
It's a welcome release quite grand.

Going home to a place of immense love,
Unlike anything experienced on earth,
And the love we experience here,
Is definitely not the first.

We have experienced that love with our loved one,
So many times before,
And when we reunite with them again,
We'll feel it again evermore.

The love we experience can never be lost,
That love is ever part of us, it becomes part of our soul,
All the love we receive and share,
Makes us stronger than we know.

Thinking that we have lost it,
Is an illusion which tests our might,
It tests our faith and inner knowing,
Until we tell negative thoughts to take flight.

We learn new ways to communicate,
On levels we had forgotten,
Where we communicate with angels, guides and loved ones,
And elevate ourselves from the downtrodden.

Janine Palmer (Silver Moon)

Tame the Ghosts

What are these ghosts of experiences past?
How long will we give them life and allow them to last?
They might whisper erroneously, that we did something wrong,
Don't allow that stagnating falsehood, to hang around too long.

We come here to have experiences, for the purpose that we learn,
This helps our soul to evolve, it's the illusions we must burn,
I speak of the illusions and the programming we are taught,
And believing we are unworthy, a misinterpretation which we bought.

That is something we should burn, we should throw it into the fire,
Break through the chains and the veil and throw them on the pyre,
We can walk out of our jail cells, where we don't belong,
And step away from the mind control, of ongoing dogmatic throngs.

Tap into your wisdom, to your sacred inner truth,
Of certain thoughts and misperceptions, we must take charge of and then mute,
When you step out of the fear and the gripping mind control,
So much freedom you will feel, when you're open to your soul.

Who is the master of your path, is it someone that you fear?
Because if you have any fear of your master, it's not your master dear;
You are part of God, have no fear of who you are,
What so many are programmed to believe and fear, from God is very far.

The sacred love you come from, has no need to control you in any way,
False gods and misinformed clergy, hold way too much negative sway,
Listen to your inner voice, to your spirit and your soul,
Who will tell you that you are worthy and loved more than you know.

Janine Palmer (Silver Moon)

The Dark Will Test You

Don't you know the dark will test you?
Don't you know you can prevail?
Darkness is an indifferent teacher,
How will you trim your sail?

From where do we gather our courage?
Do we find our innate strength within?
Do we gain our power back,
When we rise above the illusion of sin?

Do we conquer so much darkness,
When we recognize our own worth?
Do we breathe new life into ourselves,
From the consciousness we rebirth?

The dark will show us things,
We will find things hidden there,
Maybe even wings we didn't know we had,
The mystery of shadow and light so fair.

Janine Palmer (Silver Moon)

hidden

There are so many things which are hidden,
So many things we just cannot see,
So many falsehoods we believe then we suffer,
And hidden is the key which would set us free.

We the hold keys which are hidden,
We hold knowledge which is hidden within,
That we always now and ever will be worthy,
We just can't hear the whispers above the din.

We hold the sacred divine undisputable truth,
Of the Word which was placed within me and you,
We are the whispers of the love of God,
And we each hold the strength to see us through.

We are students and teachers at once in the now,
We are light and shadow in motion,
We are confidence and doubt, opposing forces,
We are here by our choices all chosen.

We whisper the strains of God's love,
It flows from us like a well,
But sometimes is gets blocked with fog and mist,
The illusions of life are like hell.

But the most powerful force in creation,
Is never hidden from us,
Even though sometimes we don't see it or feel it,
That most powerful force is love.

Love is all around us,
We just need to draw it in,
And it's so much easier to do this,
When we rise above the illusion and notion of sin.

Embrace the love of God,
By embracing the love of yourself,
Embrace the love of your brothers,
Break out of your masks and your shells.

Things are hidden by veils,
But as you begin to awake,
You will begin to see that elusive key,
In your own hand for your very own gate.

Janine Palmer (Silver Moon)

The War

The spiritual war ongoing,
The test of a warrior's might,
Swirling in the mists of illusion,
The ideas of wrong and right.

And what do we give our power to?
Or do we take our power back?
What feeds off of your fear, anger or sadness?
And what is it you think you lack?

Do you realize you are all you need?
Do you realize you have gifts and knowledge untapped?
Do you share your knowledge and wisdom with your brother?
Or do you walk around with your knife or ax?

When you stand in your energetic power,
Your most powerful protection is your own love,
Your connection to the Highest Divinity,
No need to for external weapons or boxing gloves.

You possess powers which are hidden,
Tools rather than weapons perhaps,
Tools to cut away what might interfere with you,
So you can take your power back.

Tools are often extensions,
Of our power radiating out on other levels,
And it is the power flowing through it,
Which beats back all those devils.

A sword, a dagger, or an ax,
A knife, the light, or your will here,
Are tools to take your power back,
By disconnected yourself from illusion's tear.

We fight against illusions,
We fight against so many misperceptions,
We react to what we think we see,
We react to misinterpretation and our own reflection.

We believe thoughts which are not true,
We react to things rather to respond,
We go off to war without all the facts,
Staying stuck in hell and not seeing what is beyond.

We think we need weapons to fight off,
Things outside of ourselves,
When so much of what we think we see,
Are illusions to test us from hell.

When we come into right alignment,
When we rise above illusion and fear,
We are able to see beyond the hell,
Of this lower dimensional reality unclear.

When we reconnect with the love of our Sacred Heart,
We raise the collective vibrational level,
When we share that love with our brother,
We then rise above so many false devils.

When we combine our light as a collective,
And raise the vibration of the planet too,
That is when we overcome the darkness here,
Which is ever trying to come through.

Janine Palmer (Silver Moon)

Beyond Masks & Disguise

Masks

So many masks and shields, so many walls and illusions,
Are our thoughts our idols, are we lost in confusion?
Are our thoughts right and others' thoughts wrong,
Just because we each sing a different song?

Explore the exquisite beauty of your higher self,
You have infinite gifts in you, belonging to no one else;
Do you ever feel the victim, of a game you cannot win?
And do you find you buy into, the dogmatic illusion of sin?

Some things we follow, which we think are true,
Purposefully or unintentionally, mislead me and you;
What if we all stepped out of the box?
Or took a mighty sword and shattered the locks…

Shatter the locks and tear open the veil,
Remove our worn-out masks, in order to prevail;
We prevail by remembering, the truth of our Divine Source,
We take our power back, by sailing our own course.

When you see another blinded, by the illusion of their mask,
Inquire whether you can help them, you simply need to ask;
Some will be open to becoming free,
Others will continue, to identify with 'you against me.'

Living behind the mask, is very much like being asleep,
Disconnected from Divine Source, to an unfortunate degree,
Identified with separation, and thoughts of being right,
Ever and ever defensive, and always ready to fight.

Some sit in the pews, with their Holy Bible in hand,
While judging those around them, ignoring their Lord's command,
To recognize divine truth, is to recognize we are One,
That were all brilliant sparks, of the light of the divine sun.

To reconnect with our compassion, is to live in a state of grace,
Is to shine the light of the All to everyone, a reflection of God's face;
Honor your Holy path, and that of your brother too,
Neither of you is right or wrong, to thine own self be true.

Janine Palmer (Silver Moon)

Vortex of Destruction

Destruction comes in many ways,
And sometimes it's not all bad,
Sometimes things need to be cleared away,
We're not meant to hold onto everything we had.

Some things fall apart for our learning,
So new things can fall into place,
They are tests which teach us to rise above,
To rediscover our divinity and grace.

To learn to be in gratitude,
For blessings which always abound,
And to release anger, guilt and sorrow,
For our inner wisdom to be found.

We won't find what we need,
Outside of us anywhere,
Those things are only reflections,
Pointing us back to our inner lair.

The things we recognize in others,
In ourselves we will also discover,
Because all the beauty we think we see,
Is in us which we need to uncover.

When we lift the veil of illusion,
Of falsehoods, pain and lies,
We will discover indescribable love and beauty,
Is hidden beneath our disguise.

We all wear masks here on earth,
Until we realize their stifling presence,
We take our power back when we remove them,
And feel the beauty of divine resonance.

Janine Palmer (Silver Moon)

his Mask

He definitely didn't like it,
When I boldly removed his mask;
He didn't like having that part of him exposed,
To uncover an area of some lack.

To reveal parts of himself,
Which needed to be healed,
To unveil a part of himself,
Which shows how his own happiness he steals.

He is in the habit of hiding insecurities,
Behind a mask of pomp and sass,
Which he was slowly beginning to see,
Kept coming back to kick him in the ass.

The boy in him needed healing,
He wanted the world to think,
He was a brave and valiant warrior,
But from his own cup he could not drink.

The parts of himself he did not like,
Were the parts he strengthened by force,
And by hiding the unhealed pain,
He severely altered his own sacred course.

In life we must be humble.
We must learn humility on our knees,
We must let go of false self-image,
We must release the ideas of these.

We must stop force feeding to the world,
An image which isn't true,
For when we reveal our true soul to the All,
Our true beauty will shine through.

Janine Palmer (Silver Moon)

Emotions & Memories... or Demons & Ghosts?

Sometimes emotions are triggered from memories,
How do we allow them to make us feel?
Are those emotions partial memories?
Is the way they feel illusion, or is it real?

Is the pain something you still carry?
Which you should have released so long ago?
Is it because you're not understanding what you learned from it?
In order to release what blocks your flow?

Maybe we get stuck in patterns,
Maybe we believe false thoughts which are lies,
Maybe we haven't processed and released them,
And so we hide behind masks and disguise.

Are the memories painful like ghosts of the past?
Do we allow them to haunt our days?
Do they seem like demons which are trying to teach you something?
But you can't get out of your own way?

Our emotions are very curious things,
They are guides which help us know we're alive,
It's up to us how we perceive and process them,
As to whether we suffer or we thrive.

Do they show us how we feel about something?
Maybe only to a degree…
Because we react or respond due many things,
Which allows us or prevents us from seeing.

We might react to part of the information,
Because we don't have all the facts,
So we mistakenly assume partial truth or falsehood,
As fact not knowing we are in lack.

We might be running programs,
Which cause us to react in certain ways,
We might have expectations about things,
Which is like digging our very own graves.

So our emotions are sort of a sign post,
If we are open to certain things,
Like the fact that we are here to learn something,
And to know better next time if it stings.

But we don't need to build a fortress,
Around our heart with steel armor,
Because most of the time we misperceive,
And people don't mean to harm us.

It's the ego which thinks it's hurt,
It's the ego which wants control,
It's the ego which keeps us stuck in life,
In pain because it blocks our flow.

Emotions can be likes demons,
When we suffer because of them,
Because we believe falsehoods and illusions,
But these are opportunities for awakening to begin.

Will you allow your emotions to be a demon?
Or will you view them as a guide?
Will you take what you learned from an experience?
Or will you allow it to cause you to hide?

You are in charge of your destiny,
You are in control of choice,
It's free will which teaches us to sink or swim,
Will you listen to your higher or lower voice?

Janine Palmer (Silver Moon)

Connections

The pain of losing a friend new or old,
Due to reactions of perceptions of things,
And the pain and the armor and closing off,
Because of the challenges life continues to bring.

To lose a connection once important,
Over something so small it seems,
To change our perspective in an instant,
Due to the lashes of words as they sting.

Like a target are we as they're hurled,
Unkind things which aren't even true,
And our reaction and explosion of defensive ire,
Toward a stranger we thought we knew.

How can a being who we have loved so deep,
Change into something so distant and unknown?
And how do we communicate with their idea of injury,
When such nastiness is now being shown?

And what if our apology means nothing to them?
And what if no harm was intended,
And what do we do with this once thriving friendship,
Which now hangs from a noose so suspended?

We learn from the challenges of life school,
We see something in the mirror they present,
We might see parts of ourselves which need healing,
While each of our perspectives we hold with intent.

We only understand things from our perspective,
Another's perspective is unclear,
And what muddies the waters of everything,
Are old wounds and patterns and fear.

And sometimes they actually push us away,
Sometimes intentionally and sometimes not,
But in any case it feels rather tragic,
When it feels like the depth of our love they forgot.

And life will deal this many times,
To see how we will react;
Will we remain calm, poised and composed?
While our character is under attack?

Just how much false accusation,
Is a being supposed to endure?
Before they feel compelled to disconnect,
To find peace, such an elusive cure.

And we go into a mode of protection,
From the things they are throwing our way,
Unkind words which cause a volatile reaction,
And the connection changes that day.

Old wounds present still unhealed,
Patterned reactions and outbursts do maim,
And now the gap has widened,
And it will never again feel the same.

Because as humans we forget to hold space,
We forget to be understanding sometimes,
We forgot a thing called compassion,
And proper communication dies on the vine.

And the love we felt deep inside,
Is something that will never go away,
But due to the unhealed wounds we hide,
The love is also hidden and buried to stay.

We become afraid to express it fully,
We become afraid to expose ourselves anymore,
Because it appears the person we trusted to honor us,
Has kicked our love out the door.

Relationships here are temporal,
They change like the seasons do too,
They will teach you and guide you and test you,
And at times they will make you feel blue.

Spirit Silver Moon

Glow

Wispy tendrils of fragrant smoke,
Wound its way up through the branches of the trees,
Carried about by the dancing spirit of ancient whispers,
Existing in and out of this dimension and upon the sacred breeze.

Together they sat beside their sacred fire,
Weaving flowers and twigs closely together,
Reminders of deep eternal love,
Then and now and forever.

And the firelight cast a magical glow,
Which was reflected there in their eyes,
Between them there were no masks present,
They shared the honesty of their souls in the absence of disguise.

So many animals were present,
In the physical and in spirit,
And messages flowed in from angels and guides,
But only for those who could hear it.

For those who were open to divine guidance,
Who had opened to awaken to awareness,
Who functioned from a higher level of love,
Having risen above ego, fear and carelessness.

Through the higher vibration of their energies,
Connected with the spirit of the trees where ancient wisdom flowed,
Creating a vortex of unconditional love anchored by their connection,
And the light of their combined energies was reflected in the fire's glow.

Janine Palmer (Silver Moon)

When They Fall

It's interesting when the masks fall off,
And what they then reveal,
And the illusions you had of happiness,
The mask once offered and now steals.

Because the buried pain and programs,
Rear their heads and roar,
And hurl you through something unexpected,
Through their skeleton's closet doors.

Some things we can deal with,
And other things we cannot,
Because we can't fix anyone else's issues,
And previous knowledge of it we had not.

We are there for reasons,
On the path of someone else,
Experiences might teach us to stand in our power,
And not get drawn into their hell.

Who is the warrior of you my friend?
Who pulls your puppet strings?
You are not beholden to anyone,
Who temporarily makes your heart sing.

Don't be shocked when their mask falls off,
Don't expect anyone else to be able to heal your pain,
But always be aware of what you're learning,
And the enlightenment you continue to gain.

Just because a person can't break free of patterns,
Doesn't give them license to abuse you,
When their pain and anger leak out,
It might be an opportunity for healing to come through.

You decide how people are allowed to treat you,
Are you open and honest, or are you vague?
Do you release what no longer serves you?
Or carry it around like a plague?

Do you function in highest integrity,
In everything you do?
To the best of your ability,
Do you allow God's love to come through?

Do you twist things all around,
To divert them from yourself?
Not wanting to take any responsibility,
For your self-created hell.

But your hell when you don't heal it,
Can leak out and burn those you love,
And because of your bloody armor,
You can't hear the voice of the dove.

Do you hear the pain in another?
Which on some level you have created,
Or do you bend over backwards in denial,
Until the shit storm has abated?

Warrior up and bear it,
The consequences of your actions,
Be prepared to deal with the fallout,
Which comes in the form of reactions.

Don't be the king or queen of denial,
Be honest in its face,
Because that is the power and might of truth,
Which stands strong in its own grace.

Janine Palmer (Silver Moon)

Light Through the Cracks

Druid Priest

He breathed in the air of nature,
The healing fragrance of the trees,
He reveled in their abundant beauty,
And he whispered his gratitude on the breeze.

He was summoned to meet an elder guide,
A message he was called to receive,
Because of his open heart and soul,
Because his inner truth had risen above belief.

He walked through the woods to an ancient cave,
He walked under the sheltering canopy of leaves,
He was a teacher and messenger for the light of the world,
And he'd been opened in love to receive.

Doing ongoing work for the greater good,
Flowing through the illusion of time,
To bring light into the darkness of hell,
To rise above fear, back to love sublime.

He entered the cave of enlightenment,
For the guidance he would receive there,
And he greeted his old, familiar friend,
Who lived in the Dragon's Lair.

This dragon had entered this lower realm,
To keep a close eye on the progress of man,
Of our progress in evolving out of the darkness,
And in our own power and truth to stand.

To realize we must disengage,
From ego's nefarious rule,
To be aware we don't need to be in control of things,
Because when we do we become a fool.

When we realize no one can take our truth,
That no one can take our power,
We then lose the illusion of any need to control others,
Our soul opens and blossoms and flowers.

The ancient and wise old dragon,
Gave the old Druid a knowing grin,
He laughed with a tiny puff of smoke,
And said, "My dear friend, let us begin."

They sent up a prayer to the Creator,
To the Creative Spirits and Angels of Light,
They drew in Universal healing light energy,
And together they raised the collective vibe.

The dragon whose name was Twilight,
Thanked the Druid for his work for the Divine,
He told him of areas where darkness was rampant,
Because mankind falsely believed so many lies.

He told him how darkness was posing,
As a source of light and salvation for man,
And there were so many masks on this material plane,
That most did not know where to stand.

Darkness was using religions and the Beloved name of the Christ,
And man's lowly little ego, which always wants to be right,
To create separation and fighting between them,
So they missed the deeper meaning and continued to fight.

They mistreated their brothers and sisters,
They mistreated the animals too,
They mistreated their earth mother who sustained them,
And the gate to the light they could not get through.

The Druid often spent quiet time in reflection,
In a place of holy prayer,
To call in legions of angels,
To aid mankind through the mazes down here.

And each man and woman will open,
To the truth and the light from within,
Only when they were ready,
And their soul's ascension will begin.

Only when they'd had enough suffering,
Only then would they begin to see the light,
Only when they had been cracked open here,
Would they begin to separate wrong from right.

But wrong and right is duality,
It's part of illusion's dark snare,
To realize it's not about wrong and right,
But about experiences for evolving while here.

The dragon reminded him of Thought Forms,
And the dungeons of hell they create,
And about releasing those false entities,
To the light and then open the gate.

To open the gate to our inner self,
To open to our truth within,
Truth does not lie outside of ourselves,
And when discovered, the true journey begins.

Janine Palmer (Silver Moon)

Smokey Tendrils

The fire burned its beauty,
Breathing out into the night,
The energy of transmuting,
To another level of light.

On silvery smoky tendrils,
She released to the ethers beyond,
All that she threw into the fire,
And she could feel her spirit respond.

She threw in expectations,
Of anything going a particular way,
She threw in old pain and resentment,
Things holding her back would no longer hold sway.

She threw in anger and sadness,
She threw in unforgiveness too,
She wanted to open her soul to receive,
For universal healing energies to come through.

She created a space for healing,
But first she had to let go,
Of things which no longer served her,
To open to things she didn't yet know.

Because learning new things is remembering,
Things which we already know,
When we release the blocks and the programs,
The blessings begin to flow.

She danced through the smoke in gratitude,
She sent up her prayers to the divine,
She cut the chords to anything negative,
And nurtured the connection to the sacred vine.

The trees around her were happy,
They whispered to her in ancient song,
She connected with the love of the Creator,
To the Source which she ever belonged.

Janine Palmer (Silver Moon)

Druid Tower Library

The Druid is a part of her being,
Part of her essence divine,
Part of her beautiful ancient soul,
Brought back with her here this time.

She brings with her part of Egypt,
She breathes the goddess's breath,
She came here as a divine scientist,
A teacher of compassion to do her best.

Always connected with spirit,
Whether, native or nun or witch,
High priestess, great mother or virgin
It's divinity she comes here with.

The high priestess sits in her library,
Where she studies the ancient tomes,
She studies ancient wisdom in the afternoon,
Until she hears the church bell tone.

She serves humanity daily,
She is a healer in her land,
She weaves in love with her compassion,
To nurture her fellow man.

She is a teacher and a gentle guide,
She is beauty and grace in flow,
She opens the hearts of so many,
And their love for her they always show.

She does not judge the masses,
She leaves that to their free will choice,
The consequences of their actions,
Will be their judgmental voice.

She teaches them to be in awareness,
Of the knowledge that they gain,
And to hold nothing against themselves,
And their judgment to restrain.

They should hold nothing against another,
To stay away from that prison cell,
And if they do they will steer clear,
Of so much self-made hell.

In her tower library of knowledge,
Where her wisdom seems to grow,
She listens to the guidance of the higher ones,
Which causes her spirit to glow.

On her lap a familiar friend,
Who purrs with love for her there,
Who balances her energy nicely,
Our energy we are meant to share.

Janine Palmer (Silver Moon)

The Cross

What is the cross of falsehood?
So much of the world bears?
Why do they adopt and carry the lies?
Why do they fall into the snare?

They fall because they are sleeping,
They fall because of the veil,
They fall because they forgot their origins,
Their eyes are closed to the sacred rail.

Too busy defending what they think is correct,
Too busy fighting with their brother,
Too busy trying to prove they are right,
Too busy to realize they are the other.

Thankfully some of us are awakening,
We hear the call of our soul,
We feel the love that is everywhere,
And then we begin to blossom and grow.

We awaken to our God-self,
We recognize God within,
Not an idea found in a book or a building,
Who is not concerned with sin.

Sin is a diabolical idea,
Sin is an idea of fear,
Sin is a tool used by darkness,
And when we believe that lie, our focus is unclear.

Love is the only truth of this world,
Love interwoven in the mists,
Love which comes from us,
When we embrace our soul's true bliss.

Look for love all around you,
You will see it everywhere,
Let the love flow from your heart,
Be a warrior of love, if you dare.

Janine Palmer (Silver Moon)

The Bell

Is it the substance which rules you?
Or is it some form of lack?
Is it a mask you hide behind?
Or is it a knife in your back?

Are you really a victim?
Or do you believe the lies?
Did you willingly give your power away?
Do you always wear that disguise?

Do you have any control,
Over yourself at all?
Have you or have you not,
Learned to rise after a fall?

Do you think it might be time,
To stop swimming in your own hell?
Are you waiting for a sign?
Are you waiting for the sound of the bell?

Don't destroy anything further,
Throw yourself out of the nest,
Trust that your wings will support you,
It's just another test.

The bells are the situations in life,
Which rock your world and scream to 'wake',
But we don't hear the bells behind masks and illusions,
Because we're blinded and our self we forsake.

So many are blinded by substance abuse,
So many are controlled by things,
Only when you've been thrust to your knees and cracked open,
Can you let go of the things to which you cling.

To sit there with that bottle,
Or pipe or glass in hand,
And give your power to something outside of yourself,
Is to fall on your sword where you stand.

Listen for the bells in life,
Which try to call you home,
But you must walk away from those demons,
Or in misery will you will continue to roam.

Janine Palmer (Silver Moon)

Energy Vampire

Because of pain and hardship,
And pain carried and not released,
Existing in a place of fear and lack,
And of their own happiness they are a thief.

And so they might try to draw you in,
To a place where they can take,
Your energy then to strengthen themselves,
With no thought or care for your sake.

Stealing any energy or power,
From someone else which is not their own,
Is not okay on any level,
And for it they must atone.

The karma they don't believe in,
The karma they don't respect,
Will deliver a taste of their own creation,
And they will learn from their own neglect.

There are spiritual laws which govern,
Which are higher than any human being;
Because of their lust for power they take,
And there are consequences they are not seeing.

You can take your energy back,
Claim it with valiant force,
Call in legions of divine angels,
To assist you on your course.

You have the power here and now,
To call your energy and power back,
Cut cords, tear up contracts and disconnect,
From any lower vibrational attack.

Whisper encouragement to yourself,
You have within you all you need,
There is no need to stand there injured and weak,
No one has the right to make you bleed.

Janine Palmer (Silver Moon)

Things Married

Was it meditation, a dream or a vision?
When she entered into the cave?
Was he a knight in shining armor?
Or would his mask fall off to reveal the knave?

Some of his qualities here so gallant and true,
His energy nurtured her and drew her near,
But his old pain, scars and demons would make her question,
How a connection between them could conquer old fears.

She could offer him her divine love,
Perhaps like nothing he'd experienced before,
But she could not fix his issues for him,
Only he could walk through that door.

And if he did not or could not find,
A way to release the pain buried under his armor,
To peel away and release the layers torturing him,
He would eventually push her away and harm her.

Each being upon this planet,
Must find a way to heal the wounds they carry,
Or more pain and suffering would be created,
Which would separate things which were married.

Things which are married together,
May not be a perfect match,
Especially when there are doors still locked,
And the keys are lost to the latch.

We are the keys to our latches,
We all hold the answers within,
And when we detach from old thoughts and embrace it,
Then our healing can now begin.

Janine Palmer (Silver Moon)

Our Own Love & Trust

Through healing comes transformation,
When we are cracked open then the light comes in,
And when we release old and useless burdens,
Our true journey can begin.

The journey is always unfolding,
The journey strengths us thus,
The journey will knock us down to find our wings,
So we can rise through to our own love and trust.

The one we need to trust is our self,
But we must be open to listen,
Because new pearls of wisdom are always reflected,
Like the dew of each new day which glistens.

To fill ourselves with divine love,
And then to share it and give it away,
To lift our brethren as they heal,
Through the truth and the light and the way.

The truth is always within us,
It is not fully found anywhere else,
Outside of us are only partial truths,
And that is not where we should dwell.

Dwelling in erroneous falsehoods,
Only serves to keep man stuck,
Pointing their fingers in righteous judgment,
And passing judgment's buck.

Partial truths will only limit mankind,
Who is always connected to the vine,
Unless and until we disconnect from,
The idea of yours and mine.

We are a collective tribe,
And we recognize it through love and trust,
When we pierce through the fog and the veil,
And break through illusion's dark rust.

Janine Palmer (Silver Moon)

Torrent

A torrent of love and blessings,
Are ever on their way to you,
But you must release any old pain or fears,
To allow them to come through.

You must release any thoughts of guilt,
Which can only be forgiven by you,
In order to sweep out the old,
For the new sprouts to grow through.

The things we keep holding onto,
The things to which we cleave,
Which bock our energy from flowing,
And what we can achieve.

A torrent of pain and anger,
Or torrent of love and peace,
Everything needs to flow,
What energy do you release?

A torrent of unforgiveness,
Is like quicksand in a cell,
A torrent of love's forgivenss,
Will flush you right out of hell.

Flow upon the river of this life,
In gratitude as you can,
Let things flow through and not get stuck,
Lifting your soul, your tribe, your clan.

Janine Palmer (Silver Moon)

Tangled Threads

Our connections here are many,
Some give, some test, some take,
Some create joy, some create pain,
All for experience's sake.

Sometimes the threads get tangled,
Sometimes they must be severed,
Some are pure and true,
Some are cheeky and clever.

When things are in knots or tangled,
We must be patient and be still,
We must thoughtfully work the knots loose,
Exercising respect by our free will.

Sometimes things seem to get mixed up,
Between our heart and our mind,
Sometimes we wear our blinders,
And meet ignorance in kind.

But tangles can be worked through,
Do we comb through them or do we cut them?
Do we hide away in fear?
Or do we let new rays of light in?

The wound is where the light enters us,
We are cracked open in so many ways,
And what we find when we are on our knees,
Are tools to guide us through the maze.

Our individual journeys,
And the things which we will find,
When we open to our truth within,
Will loosen falsehoods and unbind.

When we cut away the old threads,
Of things which no longer serve,
We become free to accept new threads of love,
Which nurture and heal our verve.

Janine Palmer (Silver Moon)

Freedom Through Awakening

Clearly

Clearly you have lost something,
Is it a connection to love so deep?
Clearly there is sadness in your heart,
Is it pain which keeps you from sleep?

Do you replay those repetitive loops,
Of perceived mistakes through your mind?
Has your connection to your true self disappeared?
Does it block your energy, keeping you stuck and blind?

Clearly you could use some healing,
To balance the parts of yourself,
Clearly you have been putting it off,
Too focused on the sadness and hell.

Remember that hell is a creation,
Which is made exclusively by you,
If you decide you really don't like it,
There is something which you should do.

You should be in gratitude for the lessons,
Be in gratitude for the wisdom gained,
Release then what no longer serves you,
And tune into what can be gained.

You hold the keys to your freedom,
From perceptions, falsehoods and lies,
Your higher self is the wisdom keeper,
Which sees through the masks and the guise.

Restore yourself to power,
A magnificent creative force,
Rise like a Phoenix from the ashes,
Fling open so many new doors.

Janine Palmer (Silver Moon)

Within or Without

Will you hold your pain within?
Forever and a day?
Or will you agree to release it,
And greet a brand new day?

Will you take your power back?
Or will you remain in your cell?
Will you open up your heart?
And detach yourself from your hell?

Will you walk out of your prison?
The one you created here?
To greet the world in wonder?
And the love which you hold dear?

Will you embrace forgiveness?
Will you now let go of the pain?
Will you open your mind to knowledge?
And be in gratitude for blessings gained?

Janine Palmer (Silver Moon)

Shadows from the Tree of Life

The tree of life grows beneath the light,
Of a mysterious magnificent Source,
So as the light shines through its branches,
We find shadows there of course.

We must navigate through the shadows,
And the light nurtures the tree,
While the roots benefit from the darkness,
The light is ever free.

There are mysteries there within,
As the secrets ever unfold,
We must sift the wheat from the chaff,
Which is more complicated than we're told.

We must find the truth between,
The branches of shadow and light,
We must know that all will be well,
And remember that day is connected to night.

See clearly with your inner sight,
That many things are not what they seem,
And use your divine intuition,
Then enlightenment you shall glean.

Janine Palmer (Silver Moon)

Poison Wine

The things we draw into our beings,
Our mysterious sacred space,
The things we believe and then suffer,
Things which nurture us or disrupt our grace.

The things we are presented with,
The things which we imbibe,
The things which are not our truth,
The things which separate us from our light tribe.

We drink of things we are offered,
In curiosity from time to time,
Searching for answers and acceptance,
But sometimes we drink from poisoned wine.

The poison wine could be anything,
Disguised as truth somehow,
But the truth is not outside yourself,
It's time to awaken now.

The beauty you are inside of you,
Is beauty you might not yet see,
In searching for our true self,
We often give our power away to find we are no longer free.

So life will crack us open,
To let the light deep inside,
That is the moment we begin to heal,
It's the moment we no longer hide.

To step out of that box which binds us,
To shred it and burn it with our power,
Is when we begin to open to our inner truth,
The unfolding of divinity's flower.

But we must let go of our thoughts about things,
We must let go of the notion of being right,
We must disengage from falsehoods and dogma,
To see the true light in our brother's eyes.

We can't always see our brother through scripture,
Because it is connected to the veil,
Truths woven in with falsehoods,
Can you see the deeper truths, hidden behind the nails?

Some believe the fairy tales,
And insist they are the truth of all,
And that will be the notion of belief,
Shortly before they fall.

Only when you awaken to your divine spark,
To recognize your sacred divinity within,
Will you stop drinking from the poison wine,
And the gross ongoing misinterpretations of sin.

Take a step back from the illusions,
Continually playing on life's movie screen,
To see the truth behind the lies,
And therein lies the freedom you shall glean.

The kingdom within is where you shall find,
The truth of your magnificence and of your Creator,
That's when you step will out of illusion,
To move back to love from illusion's gate.

For the Love of God (The God who does not use fear to manipulate man)

Janine Palmer (Silver Moon)

Raven Wood

He spoke to the trees of a goddess,
He said she'd awakened to her course,
To remember her sacred origins,
To assist humanity to open new doors.

He told them the good news of her spirit,
And in gratitude they happily rejoiced,
For they knew of the depth of importance here,
Of the rebirth of the Divine Feminine voice.

She would be a messenger and a healer,
She had studied and opened and learned,
She had remembered humanity's divine origins,
And into the fires the dross would be burned.

She was to open man's heart in awakening,
Her weapon was her compassionate flame,
She was to remind man of his magnificence,
And to step out of ego, judgment and blame.

She was to heal their hearts with their own truth,
To cast the lies of sin and hell into the fire,
To rise above darkness's programming,
And place the burdens and pain on the pyre.

To rise above man-made religions,
To a direct connection with God,
To lift the veil and open their hearts,
To allow their souls to rise above lower thoughts.

To move toward ascension in oneness,
To flow with the collective consciousness stream,
To step into their own sacred hearts,
To their kingdom within, and their own dreams.

To teach them that the truth is within them,
It is nowhere outside of their being,
Except in the love in this world that is shared,
It's the ego and illusions which keep man from seeing.

She knew of the importance to restore balance,
Between the Divine Feminine and Masculine too,
In order to rise out of this hellish state,
Which darkness has kept us tied to.

Janine Palmer (Silver Moon)

The Awakening

When she opened her heart and soul,
When she stepped out of earthly illusion,
She began to remember her origins,
Which blew the doors off of so much confusion.

When she recognized God the Creator,
That He/She created so many things,
She stepped out of any arrogant notion,
That humans are the only relevant beings,

New worlds began to open to her,
New visions began to appear,
And she knew she was never alone,
She was surrounded by beings so dear.

What exists around her is amazement,
No words could begin to describe,
But most do not even see it,
Disconnected as they are from their light tribe.

Most do not feel it,
They don't remember from whence they came,
They are caught up in earthly illusions,
Of ego and pointing fingers in blame.

But she has had an awakening,
She has opened up her mind,
She has opened her heart and soul to truth,
And left so many falsehoods behind.

Janine Palmer (Silver Moon)

Soul Song

Something whispered to her from the woods,
Something familiar and soft and sweet,
She followed it, slightly intrigued,
Wondering what curiosities she would meet.

She stepped softly on the forest path,
The earth supported her every step.
She gazed all around her in wonder,
She heard whispers right and left.

She came upon a tree stump,
Where she sat and closed her eyes,
Then she understood the whispers,
Came from her soul without disguise.

She had let down her walls of illusion,
Like she sometimes let down her hair,
What she heard was her heart and soul speaking,
From higher levels she'd previously been unaware.

They called her back into nature,
To be reconnected, free and in tune,
Because she had connected to higher consciousness,
To be a voice for the collective very soon.

She breathed in the scent of the beautiful trees,
In gratitude she grounded to the earth,
She released what did not serve her,
And her higher Self there she rebirthed.

She freed herself on many levels,
She opened up to her heart and soul,
To the wonder of things previously unseen,
To the brilliance of the collective glow.

She shattered and broke through the veil,
She opened to her own truth inside,
She accessed another dimension,
Masks and illusions she would no longer abide.

Janine Palmer (Silver Moon)

Sleeping Beauty Awakened and Rising

I am noticing a pattern here,
As so many goddesses now awake,
They hear the call of their deepest soul,
And they answer it for their own sake.

And so many men, their partners,
Seem to resist it like the plague,
Not ready or willing to step out of their boxes,
Boxes of pain and fear and rage.

So many goddesses are noticing,
That their men would rather swim in their dark pain,
Perhaps too fearful to step out of their cells,
And into the light of the fire unrestrained.

Many put their women down,
They shut them out and to substances they cling,
To their thought forms and preconceived ideas,
Shutting out the blessings she would bring.

Not all men stay in their caves,
So many are healers, warriors and sages,
Many have heard the call of their souls,
And they carry on important work through the ages.

Some of them support their goddesses,
And we are ever so thankful for that,
As in unison we work to restore balance,
We all wear coats of many colors and many hats.

There are those who choose to remain asleep,
While the world just passes them by,
Those who can't seem to disengage from fear,
When programming and conditioning are the lies.

But that is part of their journey,
So wish them well and just walk on,
Because in your heart there is divine treasure,
And you sing it as your very own song.

Janine Palmer (Silver Moon)

Into Knowing, Beyond Belief

Death Rattle

A death rattle sounded deep in my being,
And it was a very good thing,
When I let go of what didn't serve me,
How my soul really started to sing.

The life I once knew was shattered,
By events along my path,
That reality was gone now,
And I would never get it back.

But the opportunities which unfolded,
And the lessons that I learned,
Opened so many new doors for me,
For what I lost I did not yearn.

Life blew out the windows,
Of my tidy little house,
It made me feel small and insignificant,
Like a tiny little mouse.

It made me pull up my boot straps,
It made me search very deep within,
To find answers to mysterious questions,
And disconnect for the illusion of sin.

I discovered, oh what a revelation,
That what I'd been taught to believe was so wrong,
And due to the depth of truth of resurrection to such a degree,
My heart now sings a new song.

I learned some of life's deep mysteries,
So beautiful to behold,
Of healing and ancient wisdom,
Which can't be bought or sold.

Knowledge once gained must ever be shared,
We mustn't keep it to ourselves,
Buried deep within us is treasure so dear,
The deeper we must delve.

I'm speaking of the kingdom within,
I had to die a little to find,
I had to detach from thought forms and ego,
And leave the pain behind.

I experienced baptism by fire,
From the ashes I rose again,
I rose above so many false beliefs,
And erroneous notions of sin.

I discovered we come here to learn,
How to love our brother or sister so true,
And we must never endeavor to judge him or her,
Or else we're a selfish and ignorant fool.

If we judge we are ruled by our ego,
And rarely does it serve,
It challenges our higher self,
And disrupts our radiant verve.

To die to the old and be reborn to the new,
Is ever our purpose here,
To let go of what does not serve,
Will help us to be more clear.

We must love and forgive and accept ourselves,
And others as they are,
And our journeys of ascension will shine,
Like the brightest star.

Janine Palmer (Silver Moon)

Song of the Divine

Where do we fit in the mists,
Of history and the Divine Plan?
Will we be swept away by illusion,
Or will we take a stand?

Will we breathe in Divine Breath,
Or the smog of illusion and lies?
Will we stumble over man's chains,
Or will we break free of those ties?

What if we saw through the veil,
If we knew about God's own spark?
Buried and hidden within us,
Waiting to come out of the dark.

What if our inner knowing,
Which is the Kingdom with,
That vessel of Sacred Wisdom,
Was revealed to us once again?

Would we recognize the good in our brother,
In our neighbor and sister so fair?
Would we know that we are not separate,
Would the war and strife then end there?

Would we do away with our ideas
About who is right and wrong?
Would we view the world through Divine eyes?
Would we begin to sing a new song?

Janine Palmer (Silver Moon)

To Question, To Seek

She said, For so long as I have been a seeker,
For so long I continue to see,
That those who have not suffered much,
Seem to have no reason to question what they believe.

As they go along their paths in this life,
Thinking they are separate from their brother,
Going against their scriptures standing in judgment,
Falling out of love with one another.

The judgment that you stand in,
Whether you realize you're doing it or not,
Might be due to the falsehoods you believe,
Guiding you away from love due to your thoughts.

Our suffering is what cracks us open,
For the light to then shine in,
To illuminate our truth inside,
For our awakening to begin.

To realize we are always worthy,
It's darkness which tricks us into thinking we're not,
Due to misinterpretations of scriptures,
And the falsehoods we unknowingly bought.

When we recognize our God spark,
The light of God within ourselves,
That is when our ascension begins,
And we rise out of man-made hell.

Organized religions here,
Serve a purpose to a point,
Until we reconnect with our higher selves,
And the Christ Consciousness then anoints.

Janine Palmer (Silver Moon)

Iron Stone

Who is it that can pull the iron from the stone?
Be it a sword or something else...
Who can separate the spirit from matter?
Or shall we say, the heaven from the hell...

A curious mixture to be sure,
For spirit to descend here into matter,
Where it is veiled, obscured and blinded in darkness,
And consumed by ego and incessant mind chatter.

It enters though a veil of forgetting,
It forgets its origins Divine,
It forgets its utter magnificence,
Ensnared in this illusion of time...

It battles and struggles through mind games,
Through illusions of wrong and right,
It mistakenly thinks it's a worthless 'sinner',
Due to programming from believing false lies.

It becomes an initiate of a Mystery School,
When it finally begins to awaken,
It's a student of this physical school of earth,
And it's Self must not be forsaken.

For within the physical being,
Is a brilliant spark of the Divine,
A pinpoint of Light it will finally see,
Which will guide it in from the night.

It's time to awaken, my darlings,
It's time to return to the Truth that is You,
You evolve by rising out of the ashes,
But your Divinity will see you right through.

It's time now to forgive things and people,
The illusions you decided to 'believe',
It's time again to love your True Self,
For your Ascension to be achieved.

Janine Palmer (Silver Moon)

Whispers of Destiny

The whispers of destiny,
Of things preordained,
The lessons and experiences,
The losses, the gains.

The strength of our character,
Fortitude and depth,
Shifting through the chaff,
To the treasure that's left.

Who do we start out as?
Who do we become?
Are we all separate?
Or are we all one?

Do we seek the brilliant experience of love?
Do we understand, as below so above?
Is forgiveness a part of our lives we weave in?
Do we finally accept the illusion of sin?

How we treat others is a testament bold,
Which reveals if our heart is of ice or gold,
Do we lighten our load or do we carry the weight?
What if our burden won't fit through the gate?

What if our teachers were pleased with our growth?
With the light and the dark and what we learn from them both?
What if illusions were finally laid bare?
And for nothing but love should we have a care.

Janine Palmer (Silver Moon)

Power to heal

What power have we to heal?
On many levels the bodies we have,
To re-establish the balance needed,
How do we create the healing salve?

The spiritual and the physical,
The mental and emotional too,
To balance all the bodies,
Is to allow healing to come through.

To release what no longer serves you,
To replace it with self-love,
Is to shed the old to make room for the new,
As below now so above.

And to give ourselves permission,
Not to hold anything against ourselves,
To forgive ourselves and others,
To release ourselves from hell.

To rise above illusions,
To stop reacting to falsehoods now,
To stop giving our infinite power away,
To stop fighting and live in the now.

To stop worrying about the past and the future,
To live in the now right here,
Is to take back your power and begin to create,
A life of love which is free of fear.

Fear is the illusion.
Fear is the crafty lie,
Fear is what causes dark wars,
Here between you and I.

Darkness will ever test you,
But you are here to rise above,
When you reconnect to your divine light,
With the whispers of the raven and the dove.

Janine Palmer (Silver Moon)

By Choice

What if man were in control,
Of the beast within himself?
Instead of being a slave to it,
What if he could walk out of his hell?

That is where this life comes in,
The free will zone by choice,
How we determine what we learn from experiences,
How we create with our intention and voice.

How thoughts create our reality,
How words are types of spells,
Which can nurture and heal with compassion,
Or create suffering, pain and hell.

People's pain and darkness,
Might knock you down on your path,
It's up to you to get up and dust yourself off,
And to pull their knife out of your back.

Sometimes we have to disconnect,
Sometimes we have to detach,
Sometimes we have to slam the door,
And put in place the latch.

Everyone has to face and hopefully conquer,
The beast within themselves,
Because we have the choice here on this plane,
To exist in a place of heaven or a place of hell.

Janine Palmer (Silver Moon)

Metaphors & Deeper Truth

Dragon's Fang

He had experienced a type of debilitating loss,
He had been knocked down hard to the floor,
Because the time had come for him to be tested,
As life hurled him through unknown doors.

And because of the armor he wore,
Because of the armor he wore in place,
Because of the weight and the burden of it,
He could no longer see the light behind her face.

And so he effectively blocked out,
Anything coming his way,
He pushed away his life partner,
He would not hear what she had to say.

She tried to speak with him about healing,
She tried to speak with him about letting go,
Of things which blocked his energy,
Of the pain which blocked his flow.

So by his decisions which were fueled by fear,
And by his actions or lack thereof,
He affectively pushed and pushed and pushed away,
The love of his beautiful dove.

He made her feel unimportant,
He would not defend her honor,
So she walked away in separation,
Because life's challenges were upon her.

And so he felt so lonely,
And so he felt so cold,
And so they were disconnected,
And separately their lives would unfold.

His little dove went her own way,
She disconnected from him on her path,
Because she was blazing a trail for the greater good,
But there was something that she lacked.

She lacked a showing of affection,
She lacked the feeling of being accepted,
She lacked the feeling of support and partnership,
And she was tired of feeling rejected.

Because every soul needs nurturing,
Our souls need fuel to thrive,
And when we give love to another,
We help ourselves to survive.

She held a space of love for him,
She wanted to hurt him not,
But how to honor her and show love for her,
Seemed to be something he forgot.

Was it stubbornness or fear perhaps?
The origin of the behavior unknown,
But on her journey she blossomed,
In the love which her friends had shown.

In his resistance he had shut her out,
His old patterns and alcohol had shut her down,
But still she demonstrated care for him,
While blessings known and unknown did abound.

And then one day she discovered,
That he'd been impaled by a dragon's fang,
And he was fighting against what he couldn't face,
And limiting himself from what could be gained.

With help from his estranged little dove,
He accepted a shaman's healing stone,
And by allowing the healing of it in,
The dragon and its shadow were gone.

The dragon was there to redirect him,
The dragon was there to teach,
Even though it was initially unseen and unknown,
He could feel the grip of its teeth.

But when he allowed the healing in,
He began to take his power back,
After all the time he'd resisted it,
He had kept himself in a place of lack.

So he tipped his hat to the dragon,
And moved on now along his new path,
With the knowledge and wisdom he had gained,
A quiet warrior now no longer under attack.

Janine Palmer (Silver Moon)

Motion

Motion is a driving force, energy moves all around,
Energy is light waves, energy is sound;
The Word consists of energy, flowing from the Divine,
The energy of the Creator in everyone abounds.

There is a collective illusion,
Known to us as the veil,
And until we can learn to see past it,
We will struggle to prevail.

But the only Truth in the world,
Is the energy of Love,
It is has always come on light waves,
To mankind from the dove.

The Holy Spirit whispers,
To man about God's Love Divine,
That Love is in each and every one of us,
We are all connected to the vine.

Janine Palmer (Silver Moon)

Windows and Doors

A storm of destruction was brewing,
It came with incredible force,
It came under cover of darkness,
Rattling windows and doors.

It blew out the doors and windows,
Of my illusion's current reality,
It shattered so much I knew and held dear,
Which opened my eyes more to see.

It shattered things into oblivion,
It was a force that said to 'Awake,'
It was a force that took the illusion of power,
And a force that taught me, my power to take.

It forced me into acceptance,
Because surrender is ever a key,
It directed me to look within,
To the treasures there I couldn't see.

It led me to discover the kingdom,
It showed me God within,
It peeled back the veil of illusion,
And showed me the falsehood of sin.

As to the doors which destruction had taken,
And the windows I could no longer see,
I now found appearing there upon my path,
The gift of new windows and doors just for me.

And so for that devastating destruction,
I must stand in gratitude and bow,
And tell you what you might think is a curse,
Might turn out to be a blessing somehow.

Janine Palmer (Silver Moon)

Karma

Karma, my friends, is about balance,
It's about things from experiences we learn,
Whatever we do you another,
The same experience we will earn.

It's about learning not to burn each other,
It's about learning to forgive and let go,
It's about learning walk away from negativity,
Rising to our higher light and watching our darkness go.

If we cause someone hardships,
If we cause anyone any pain,
The same will be visited upon us,
It's the only true way lessons are gained.

It's all about creating balance,
We balance karma with our love,
It's also about forgiveness,
It's not about drawing blood.

Even as we begin to understand this,
And we try to remain aware,
We will continually be tested,
It is our love we must ever share.

The key is gain awareness,
Of the higher and lower selves,
And not to store any anger and sadness,
Or judgment or un-forgiveness, upon our inner shelves.

When we get 'offended',
Sometimes we misperceive,
We might react to misunderstandings,
And in our error do we grieve.

We might lash out due to protection,
We might lash out due to fear,
We might be stuck in habits,
Which generates many tears.

The way to end such karma,
Is to forgive on so many levels,
To forgive ourselves and others,
Which casts out so many devils.

Think twice before you act out,
In mean and selfish ways,
Because the same will happen to you,
Don't get stuck in that maze.

Janine Palmer (Silver Moon)

Your Father's Armor

Is it an honor or is it a burden?
Things which are passed down,
Things we feel we must carry,
Be it armor or a crown.

Do we wear the armor with honor?
And for goodness do we stand?
Or do we wear it to protect us,
From fear and our brother man?

Do you view your father's armor,
As a trophy or as a sin?
Does it guide with ancient wisdom,
Does it hinder you or help you win?

Do you carry it out of obligation?
Do you feel it should be part of your path?
Do you display it probably with honor,
Or is it collecting dust on some old rack?

Do your father's accomplishments or expectations,
Create an idea you feel you must live up to?
Do his past failures make you determined,
To walk your own path being perfectly you?

Do you know on any level,
It's your choice whether you carry it or not?
That you are your own being on your own journey,
Even if they forgot.

Honor yourself on your mission,
As your own armor you create,
Wear it like a mantle, light and free,
Don't let it become too heavy to get to the gate.

Don't use your armor to hide away,
Don't allow it to block Love coming in,
Wear it as a statement of who you are,
And always make room for a grin.

Janine Palmer (Silver Moon)

Balance & Boundaries

It's a challenge to find and maintain balance,
It's a juggling act to be sure,
It's more about being open to healing,
Than it is about finding a cure.

To balance is also to heal,
To be open is also to grow,
To add to your knowledge base without attachment,
Invites in more wisdom than you know.

Boundaries are for your protection,
To claim and maintain your own space,
To preserve your own divine energy,
In a state of love and balance and grace.

To not allow yourself to be so drawn,
In too many directions at the same time,
To stand in your power and learn to say no,
Without feeling it's some sort of crime.

The crime is when people drain you,
Taking for themselves what your spirit can give,
These are part of the tests of life,
To gain strength in the lives that we live.

To honor ourselves with boundaries,
Which we get to set and choose,
Because our personal peace in sacred harmony,
Is a thing we don't want to lose.

Janine Palmer (Silver Moon)

Our Pain Becomes Their Power

How long is it really necessary,
To carry the remnants of pain?
Is it meant to teach you something?
Or keep you hobbled, miserable and maimed?

The thing about pain we don't realize,
As well as anger, sadness and rage,
And resentment, guilt and shame,
Is that they prevent you from turning the page.

But there is something even more sinister,
Not known on lower dimensional levels,
That beings gain power from our stuck-ness,
That lower energy fuels those devils.

It does not serve our ascension,
It does not serve our purpose here,
To remain in any victim mentality,
Or in guilt or shame or fear.

When we hold onto anger,
Resentment or sadness at length,
We remain in a type of self-made hell,
And we block the flow of our energetic stream.

Think about what you hold onto,
Whether anger, pain, guilt or fear,
Ask your higher self what illusions you should release,
So you can fully experience your journey here.

Surround yourself in divine love,
The love of the All you are,
Where comfort and serenity,
Are never very far.

Janine Palmer (Silver Moon)

Don't Fear Home

This place is not our true home,
It's only for us a school,
To learn to love and balance karma,
To find our God spark jewel.

This is a place of beauty,
But it is also a place of hell,
Where we need to dig deep down,
To find within us divinity's well.

To leave here should not be feared,
To return to where we came from to rejoice,
Because where we come from is truth and grace,
Where we can hear the beauty of God's familiar voice.

Such a sacrilege that we learn to fear,
And the falsehoods religions do preach,
Where mankind becomes programmed to fear,
Which separates people so far out of reach.

Fear is the illusion,
Fear is the diabolical trap,
Fear puts a person in false dread,
Of loss and change and lack.

Home is a place of immense love,
Unlike anything experienced here,
Home to the light of our soul tribe,
Where things are clear and true and pure.

Out of this lower vibrational hellish plane,
Kick your heals as you go,
Thank it for the memories,
Onto another adventure we go.

Janine Palmer (Silver Moon)

Perspectives & Treasures

Buried Treasure

There is treasure hidden everywhere,
For the curious and the meek,
It's hidden in many things,
Our purpose on earth is to seek.

Some is hidden in plain sight,
Some we have yet to discover,
Some of it is lost to time,
Some is waiting to be recovered.

Treasures are hidden between the lines of Scriptures,
Metaphors and unrecognized codes,
Some of it is in our temples,
Our bodies of light, the spirit's abode.

We might find it in our neighbor,
In our friend and our enemy too,
We might find pieces in churches,
But falsehoods we must see through.

We might find little pieces in our prayers,
And the in answers which may come,
We might find them in our hardships,
And when we come undone.

When our prayers seem not to be answered,
And we find ourselves redirected,
Some of the treasures are the greatest,
When to our purpose we are connected.

Answers come from our Sacred Heart,
And from loving and accepting ourselves,
Answers flow when we forgive everything,
And rise to higher realms.

Answers come when we release any lingering guilt,
Any shame or any fear,
Any sadness, resentment or anger,
We are purified by our tears.

The answers are precious treasures,
They are wisdom and they are keys,
They are keys to our inner kingdom,
Where divine love reigns supreme.

The treasure is in our spirit and our soul,
Connected as we are to the All,
The only way to evolve and rise,
Is to experience the effects of the fall.

Janine Palmer (Silver Moon)

Buried Cities

Cities are buried beneath oceans,
Cities are buried beneath lakes,
Cities of knowing are buried within us,
You will discover with the steps that you take.

So many things are buried,
Wisdom, knowledge and pain,
So many things to uncover,
So many answers and treasures to gain.

So many things not faced,
We bury them deep within,
Sadness unprocessed and anger,
Too painful and viewed as sin.

The only sins are illusions,
Holding us hostage at will,
Until we free ourselves from our prisons,
With our own light we ward off the chill.

Releasing things which attach to us,
Things which wrap around us and won't let go,
Which hobble and hinder and bind us,
And interrupt our flow.

Take your dagger of light,
And cut yourself free from the chains,
Cut the ropes, the chords and the shackles,
Which only you allow to remain.

Surround yourself with glowing light,
Whisper love to yourself from your own voice,
Give yourself permission to heal and grow,
Because all you unknowingly create comes from choice.

Janine Palmer (Silver Moon)

Storms

Storms blow in and shake things up,
But they bring us things we need,
They sweep out the old and they re-direct,
They rough us up and we bleed.

Sometimes they can be refreshing,
Sometimes we might be drenched,
Sometimes we get muddy and messy,
Sometimes our thirst is quenched.

Storms often create messes,
To be cleaned up and organized,
And when we weather them and give thanks,
We will soon see more clear skies.

Sometimes storms seem scary,
Sometimes we are in awe,
Sometimes we move from fear to wonder,
Sometimes blessings come with the thaw.

Some storms we need to weather,
To learn from the trail of destruction,
To rebuild whatever is needed,
To recreate from our reconstruction.

So let the rain from the storms,
Wash away any dust and debris,
Until you feel rejuvenated,
And once again feel free.

Let the storm re-connect you with nature,
With the awe that is all around,
And the beauty hidden in everything,
And with the blessings which abound.

Janine Palmer (Silver Moon)

Treasures

Through the mists of the forest,
Through the maze of the trees,
She found the beauty of the ages,
And her spirit was connected to these.

Her energy there was a blessing,
They reveled in the beauty of her light,
For the love she gave back to nature,
Was pure and true and bright.

And in the forest the Faeries played,
And in the forest music was created,
A blending of so many different sounds,
And those who could hear it were elated.

The animals liked to watch her,
Quietly where they stood,
And they loved to hear her voice when she sang,
From beneath her emerald hood.

She sang to them songs of fancy,
And her voice was something like heaven,
And upon her shoulder they would sometimes see,
Her companion there, was a raven.

The raven brought her treasures,
Which daily he would collect,
And she accepted each one with gratitude,
Never would she reject.

And she kept them in a wooden chest,
Which she stored inside a tree,
And they were the only treasures she owned,
Except for the beauty of nature and her spirit free.

Janine Palmer (Silver Moon)

Shape Shifter

Who is this intriguing being?
Of a higher vibrational level?
Seeing into other dimensions,
Light and dark and angels and devils.

Who can shift out of this temporary veil,
Who can see things from other perspectives,
Who can bring back knowledge from other realms,
For our ascension and always reflective.

A spirit walker and a light worker,
Seeing colors of auras all around,
Or the one who sees all our angels,
And our guides who ever abound.

The ones with the gifts to rise out of the clouds,
The ones who then rise above fear,
The ones here for higher purpose,
To help others open their eyes to see clear.

Be aware that many have these gifts,
They might be able to sense the way you feel,
They are empaths who can actually feel your pain,
And they can guide you to release burdens which steal.

Some can access your records for you,
Of things from your past and your future too,
Because in spirit before you came here,
You wrote down things that you would do.

We all agree to have experiences here,
Whether we deem them as good or bad,
They are simply for our learning and to evolve,
The balance between happy and sad.

We create karma here by our choices,
And we must balance that karma too,
We balance karma always with love,
Or we swim in our own toxic brew.

So do not forget you are the author,
Of the story of the book of your life,
You create with your will your experience,
With your thoughts contentment or strife.

Learn how to peel away and release the layers,
Of old pain and things which don't serve,
To clear your energy to flow freely,
To invite in the good for your radiant verve.

Janine Palmer (Silver Moon)

Celtic Breath

He told them of a goddess,
He told them of her love,
He told them of the story,
Of the raven and the dove.

As they sat around the fire,
Under the sheltering canopy of trees,
A raven appeared before him,
With a scroll wrapped up in leaves.

He opened the delicate paper,
To read the message therein,
And upon his weathered countenance,
A pleased and knowing grin.

The wizard took a hearty sip,
Of his beloved Brandywine,
And marveled at eternal connections,
Of souls connected by the vine.

He read the script to his disciples,
It was written in green ink,
Sacred words for them to ponder,
Eternal wisdom to make them think.

Delivered from a goddess,
He knew once upon a time,
She was connected to his heart,
His Beloved Brandi mine.

"In the heart lies the beauty,
Of truth from the soul,"
Were the words which danced upon the page,
Ever a widening goal.

To discover, to remember,
The truth of these words within,
Helps man disconnect from earthy traps,
Of illusions, lies and sin.

What he and the goddess were teaching,
All the truth a being ever needs,
Is found in the kingdom within,
Right where God planted the seed.

For Brandi

Janine Palmer (Silver Moon)

When Trees Speak

He found her in a hollow,
Of an ancient forest there,
She sat in the middle of a stone circle,
With a wee fire, his lady fair.

He watched her from a distance,
And he knew she spoke to the trees,
Their wise and gentle voices,
Whispered on the breeze.

A fox had come to sit with her,
In her presence the fox was serene,
Because he recognized her attributes,
She was an ancient queen.

She stroked the fox with healing hands,
She smiled at the being with love,
And next he knew, more visitors now,
A raven and a dove.

A luminescent light,
Came from the circle there,
And then he saw an angel above,
Mesmerized in wonder, he could only stare.

He felt his heart then warming,
He felt his sadness melt away,
He felt anger, guilt and shame depart,
His heart felt light and gay.

Then she turned her eyes to him,
Standing near some trees,
She smiled at him and said,
"Please join us if you please."

He found his feet and walked ahead,
To join the beings there gathered,
The animals were not frightened of him,
Onto the coals some herbs she scattered.

She took his hand in hers,
In a greeting warm and true,
She invited him to throw into the fire,
"Anything which no longer serves you."

He threw away any unforgiveness,
He threw away doubt and fear,
He threw away lack of confidence,
And he shed a little tear.

She told him he would be healed now,
To move forward on his path,
To shed his armor and throw it in,
And for nothing would he lack.

He would function at a higher vibration,
He would draw in what he would need,
And to honor himself and find love within,
Then his Divine Self would be freed.

Janine Palmer (Silver Moon)

Monumental Gauntlet

What is this twisted path we walk?
What might our purpose be?
When will we pull the veil from our eyes,
Allowing ourselves to see?

We see from a limited perspective,
We see only part of the facts,
We react with so much pain and venom,
When the complete truth we always lack.

It is a monumental gauntlet,
Sifting the wheat from the chaff,
To decipher what is really truth,
From the burdens upon our backs.

Sometimes we believe falsehoods,
And so we suffer thus,
Everything we 'believe' is not truth,
Or it would not so separate us.

We function from limited perspective,
We react to parts of what we see,
We haven't learned to detach from hell,
And move from 'I' to 'we'.

Janine Palmer (Silver Moon)

Twists & Turns

Life is a very mysterious dance,
And different steps here we learn,
Some of them we remember,
In between new moves and twists and turns.

Like a constant river ever flowing,
Like ocean waves, part of the All,
Like light illuminating the darkness,
Like how the Mystery ever enthralls.

We dance with many people,
We dance with places and things,
We learn from silence and reflection,
We learn when we teach others to sing.

We dance when we share love,
We dance when we receive,
We dance through life's experiences,
As we celebrate, cry and grieve.

As we learn to let go of pain and rise,
As we learn not to hold things against ourselves,
As we learn the value of forgiveness,
We then rise out of versions of hell.

Hell on earth takes many forms,
Depending on what we draw in or create,
Whether we give our power away,
Or take it back as the master of our fate.

Janine Palmer (Silver Moon)

Bits of Wisdom

Little pieces of treasure,
Will constantly reveal themselves,
These little bits of wisdom,
Light your way out of hell.

You will discover them unexpectedly,
In places you would not expect,
From people and situations,
In happiness and joy and strife and neglect.

They will come from different sources,
They will reveal falsehoods through their truth,
They will help you understand the gifts from change,
Whether familiar and safe or foreign and aloof.

Bits of treasure found in books,
Truth woven in with the lies,
Even when we misunderstand scripture,
Because it is in disguise.

You will recognize the treasures,
Whenever they present,
Because they will awaken in you truth and knowing,
Like light bulbs heaven sent.

Janine Palmer (Silver Moon)

Beneath the Leaves

Beneath the leaves are treasures,
Found in the dappled patterns of shade,
Treasures placed there or forgotten,
There in the tranquil glade.

Some of the branches reach skyward,
Some of them brush the forest floor,
Some of them point to secret entrances,
To other worlds through hidden doors.

A system of nature in magic,
Glowing in transformative grace,
It's where she found the most healing peace,
A place seeming outside of time and space.

The seasons showed her the flux and flow,
The seasons would change their robes,
Nothing stood still for a moment,
God's handiwork, a temple abode.

The leaves in whatever brilliant state,
Whatever color they represent,
Beneath them you could find her lying,
The most healing way her time could be spent.

Janine Palmer (Silver Moon)

A Favorable Wind

Which way do the winds blow?
What do they change and move?
What experiences make us question things?
What would be different if the other way we blew?

What directs the winds which blow us?
From whence do the storms then come?
What is behind our decisions?
Whether we stay or run?

Where does our courage come from?
Is it something by experience we create?
Does it become like a sacred mantle we wear?
When we navigate experience's gates?

Even when a stormy wind,
Destroys things in its path,
We learn when we pay attention to,
New things which grow to replace what we think we lack.

Soothing and comforting winds,
Will come and go through time,
Woven in between the gusts and gales,
And through the clouds the sun will shine.

A favorable wind is what you make of it,
It depends on what you perceive,
To figure out what you get from it,
Will determine the gifts you receive.

Janine Palmer (Silver Moon)

Mightier

What do you find is mightier,
In any part of yourself?
What is that gifted aspect,
Which helps to rise things out of hell?

I find that my pen is mightier,
Than any physical sword,
Because I am created and I am armed with,
The power and light of the Word.

The sword is always with me,
I guard it and wield it at will,
But it functions through the strokes of my pen,
When I am active or when I am still.

The gods and masters work through me,
The angels work through me as well,
Through different aspects of who I've been,
I draw from many deep wells.

Divinity is ever flowing now,
From my sword and so from my pen,
And healing messages from higher realms,
For the people do they send.

Janine Palmer (Silver Moon)

Stories, Guides & Whispers of Love

Dishonored But Not Disgraced

I went to the place of the standing stone,
Where it stands in the shadows and mists,
I was drawn there under the moonlight,
For an encounter with Destiny's gift.

A breeze like a caress swept past me,
Rustling the dark edges of my cloak,
She stepped out from behind the standing stone,
My gaze from her presence could not be broken.

Her gown caught my eyes, of shimmering white,
It sparkled like thousands of stars on high,
A frown furrowed her beautiful brow,
Which made my soul just want to cry.

I saw stories of eternity, reflected in her eyes,
A first a thoughtful expression, then so many stories to tell,
I felt tears and happiness, light and shadow,
She showed me creation, heaven and hell.

She showed me that heaven and hell, are created here by us,
By where we allow our thoughts to linger too long,
That we need to release our heavy burdens,
And listen in silence to the Angel's song.

The atmosphere crackled like radiant fire,
It was charged with mysterious breath,
Whispers of ancient knowledge were floating,
On the wings of unseen angels so blessed.

She had been dishonored by not disgraced,
She was the Divine Feminine, in the background for far too long,
She was rising out of the waters now,
Pouring from her pitcher Compassion's song.

It was time now, she said, for awareness,
Of feminine compassion and love,
To accept the Light and the Shadow,
Of the Raven and the Dove.

We must recognize and direct our focus,
On Love and things of the Light,
And not linger too long in any negative state,
And walk gracefully out of the night.

The night serves a purpose for all of us,
But we need balance with so many things,
Masculine, Feminine, Light and Dark,
Silence at times and to sing.

Janine Palmer (Silver Moon)

The Three Masters

The Raven visited her in a dream,
Or other-dimensional state,
An old friend and a messenger,
And he told her of a gate.

He delivered to her a silver key,
Encrusted with colorful jewels,
He instructed her to travel there,
To gather some needed tools.

He said, "There are three guides waiting,
They have gifts and tools for you,
Hasten there to collect these things,
To assist you in all that you do."

She took the offered silver key,
And suddenly she was there,
At the gate to an incredible place,
A forest of beauty so rare.

Three Masters greeted her warmly,
"We're so pleased that you have come,
There are things we would like to share with you,
Because of all you do and all you have done."

"Because you have shared your compassion,
With any and all in need,
Because you give unconditionally,
And for your selfless loving deeds…"

"This forest that you are standing in,
Is one of our gifts to you,
Just use that bejeweled silver key,
For your spirit to get through."

"This is a very healing gift,
For the nurturing of your soul,
Because of your love of the forest,
And how it makes your soul glow."

"We also have a new spirit guide,
Who really is an ancient friend,
The white wolf spirit, Malik, you can call on,
When you have prayers or messages to send."

She saw a beautiful wolf appear,
And of course she remembered him now,
He'd appeared in her dreams many times,
And to her he then gave a bow.

And finally appeared an angel,
And her heart did swell with love,
This angel was her other half,
And he called her his little dove.

He told her anytime she ever feels lonely,
Disconnected or questioned her course,
To envision his mighty wings around her,
To absorb his love, such a powerful force.

Each one of them reminded her,
That she is never alone on her path,
That her thoughts can draw them to her,
And her heart and soul felt whole at last.

She knelt before them in gratitude,
A few tears trickled down her cheeks,
They embraced her with indescribable love,
And her beloved angel gave her a wink.

Janine Palmer (Silver Moon)

The Owl and the Treasure

She told the story of the owl and the treasure,
And the things hidden which remained,
And the variables and possibilities,
And courage and valor unrestrained.

She told how the owl had come to her,
And she followed him to a tree,
Hidden in the tree was a wooden box,
Beautifully carved only for her to see.

Only she could open the box,
She's stored it there for safe keeping,
Once upon a time and dimension,
Ancient wisdom which now needed speaking.

She opened the box which was full of her light,
It was the light there which was her treasure,
She absorbed the light back into herself,
Her own hidden gift of knowledge beyond measure.

Her own divine light and deep intuition,
Stored away safely for future use,
Only to be revealed to her now,
When she had risen above earthly abuse.

The abuse was part of the training,
Part of paving Ascension's way,
Part of rebirthing herself from the ashes,
To rise homeward from where she was not meant to stay.

What she needed would reveal itself,
When the time and situation was right,
When she sat with silence and listened,
And reintegrated with her own divine light.

She was a messenger for the people,
Like so many who had come before,
And like so many others here doing the work,
To open more to divinity's door.

To heal the kindred with love,
To create a healing potion,
To send light from her compassionate hands,
Moving in a forward and upward motion.

Some told her she was a goddess,
She was here to bring light and hope,
She was here to slash fallacy with her mighty sword,
She was here to cut illusion's false ropes.

Divinity has tested her fiercely,
Because tests on earth do not end,
But divinity had sent her great blessings,
In the way of her kindred soul friends.

Her friends reflected her light back,
Her friends always help up a mirror,
To keep her balanced and in right awareness,
And in her heart she held them so dear.

Janine Palmer (Silver Moon)

Tea Party

In her quest for deeper connection,
Opening to what she must remember and learn,
She was taking more time to connect with her angels,
And her guides for what her heart and soul yearned.

She chose a peaceful spot in nature,
In the shade under a canopy of trees,
They were ancient mighty oaks,
Which whispered to her in the breeze.

She set up a little table there,
With a tea service and two comfortable chairs,
And she invited in a guide for higher wisdom,
Then closed her eyes to see who would appear.

She saw a vision of a beloved guide,
Ascended to higher realms and dimensions,
And he greeted her with a familiar grin,
Knowing full well the nature of her intention.

It was Merlin, dear Merlin before her,
He said, I see you have invited me to tea,
I know you have a deep question,
And from Source I was sent here to thee.

She said, Thank you for coming, I'm honored,
To be in your divine presence here now,
I'm still learning to release old pain and fears,
And would like to learn more ways how.

He said, The pain and the fears do test you,
But are they illusions or are they real?
Allow them to teach you to guide you,
You will know truth by how you feel.

If something to you feels painful,
It's asking to be heard, to communicate,
It wants and needs to be processed and released,
To clear out old energy, we always create.

Anything which feels negative or painful,
Is not really truth you see;
It's simply an experience trying to teach you something,
Glean the wisdom and release the rest to be free.

The reason it feels painful,
Is because it's not meant to be carried around,
Only when you learn to rise above,
Will joy and peace be found.

Trust your feelings and listen,
To your intuition and your inner voice,
Because all you experience on some level you invited in,
By your karma and your free will choice.

We learn by our experiences,
And by the actions of those we love,
It's your choice whether you remain in a lower vibration,
Or whether you rise above.

There are variables connected to every situation,
Which you do not know and cannot see,
But if you knew them and with compassion,
You would forgive and set yourself free.

She nodded in agreement and thanked him,
He said, Keep on doing what you do,
But don't go anywhere just yet,
Someone else would like to come though.

He left her with a twinkle,
And next who did appear?
It was the Cosmic Priest of Ancient Days,
Melchizedek was standing there.

He said, Hello my dear I am happy,
To visit now with you here,
And to thank you for the healing work you do,
For helping humanity and their illusions to clear.

I come with a simple reminder,
To allow your divinity to shine through your face,
So those who are ready to rise above,
Will know you by your eternal grace.

Don't worry about those who do not see,
The higher purpose of your calling,
Even when they treat you unkindly,
It is they who are really falling.

Many resist what they don't understand,
Not open to and learn and to grow,
And many try to destroy what they fear,
Not ready to stand in your glow.

She thanked him with a gracious smile,
She felt lighter and so deeply loved,
She loved it when the breath of Spirit,
Flew in on the wings of the Dove.

Janine Palmer (Silver Moon)

The Faerie

The faerie was going about her business,
Nurturing the plants to thrive,
When she came upon a crumpled form,
Breathing weakly and barely alive.

She sensed that the battles of life,
Had beaten this one down so low,
That her life force was but a faint memory,
And so dim now was her life's glow.

In this free will zone are participants,
From different star systems, galaxies and soul tribes,
So brave are they to come here,
To this lower vibrational hive.

To battle their way through the veils,
To climb, to fall and to weave,
To seek, to create and to remember,
To wonder, to doubt and to dream.

To be beaten down by circumstance,
By things they each do create,
To be battered through storms to strengthen them,
To be ready to go home through the gate.

And the compassion and deep love which swirls,
Throughout their beings and the atmosphere,
Intermingled with confusion, pain and fear,
And the illusion of losing loved ones so dear.

And how they want to give up the ghost,
And how they want to return home to love,
But their journey here is not yet finished,
So they look with hope to the dove.

The fairy gathered her fair friends,
She gathered wee animals from far and near,
She gathered the healing energy from the trees and flowers,
And showered the love on her dear.

And the crumpled wee lass in the meadow,
Could feel the tingling of the energy of love,
The love of a faerie barely visible,
And the power of her love was enough.

Janine Palmer (Silver Moon)

The Dragon's Wings

She observed the activity of the dragon,
She would watch it come and go,
She would watch it take off in flight,
To mysterious destinations unknown.

The dragon was so graceful,
And she wanted to come near,
But due to the great size of it,
She stayed away because of fear.

But the dragon knew she watched him,
And one day he slowly approached,
But she sensed he wouldn't harm her,
So her question she decided to brooch.

Where do you go when you fly off,
With your mighty powerful wings?
The sound they make is so beautiful,
Like whispering winds which sing.

He said, I go to share the dragon's light,
With beings where it is needed,
I absorb the light from the divine,
And into the darkness I feed it.

She asked, How do you share the light,
My brilliant and mighty friend?
He said, watch and I will show you,
A light show which never ends.

He lifted his wings to show her,
And it was a magnificent sight,
Lights of many colors swirled,
Brilliant and healing and bright.

Under the wings of the dragon,
She saw this amazing light,
When the dragon raised it's mighty wings,
It would illuminate the night.

Janine Palmer (Silver Moon)

The Goddess and the Bear

She wandered through the moonlight,
The bear was close behind,
The sacred bear never left her side,
He protected her brilliant shine.

She was the goddess of the moon,
He was sent there by the gods,
And upon her sacred space,
No un-pure thing would trod.

He was her valiant protector,
He was the bravest in the land,
The only one he would let in,
Was the one to take her hand.

He watched over her when she worked,
With those who needed to heal,
She offered the purest gentle love,
It was from grace and it was real.

But there were those who doubted,
And in darkness continued to dwell,
The bear would not allow them to draw her in,
To their private places of hell.

That was how she tried to help them,
She tried to heal them from their hell,
She taught them about awareness,
That they had choice of where they dwell.

The bear was her greatest blessing,
Her spirit animal guide,
Her delightful totem full of love,
Always by her side.

Janine Palmer (Silver Moon)

The Quickening

She paced back and forth but she was peaceful,
She would never cave in thus,
She would not allow him power over her,
It was not the way it was done.

Because a gross imbalance,
Had become a plague upon the earth,
Because man thought he was superior,
Due to the dark power of the Church.

Man under the control of darkness,
Threw his goddess into a cell,
And unknowingly sentenced all of his kind,
Into a deep and hidden hell.

But benevolent forces were looking down,
On her, because she was needed here,
And supernatural things would be called in,
When they drew the Dragon's tear.

The winds began to swirl,
She began to hear them howl,
Gray clouds were drawing closer,
Retribution would be endowed.

Suddenly her door blew open,
And she stepped out into the storm,
Where she heard the flap of mighty wings,
And her heart began to warm.

A swift and mighty dragon,
Was descending to the ground,
And she knew this was her rescuer,
Relief and hope were found.

She thought she saw the dragon grin,
When he alighted before here there,
He extended a wing toward her,
She ascended it like a stair.

The man who had imprisoned her,
Stood by with jaw open wide,
Soon he would discover,
That behind dark lies he could no longer hide.

Janine Palmer (Silver Moon)

My Raven

He is with me through my journey,
He guides me along my path,
He is a keeper of great wisdom,
He offers guidance when I ask.

The raven brings me knowledge,
He shares knowledge from realms afar,
He watches with eyes a twinkle,
Of the light from distant stars.

A messenger of the gods,
So wise in the mysterious ways,
Who can answer the deepest questions,
With a simple, knowing gaze.

Of sacred truths and knowing,
Of sacred wisdom kept safe and handed down,
The raven guards for the initiate the knowledge
Of pure spirit virgins, grails and thorny crowns.

The raven knows of the dragons,
Who men slayed in greed for magic blood,
And of unicorns of higher dimensions,
Who with the Christ have stood.

But lower man knows nothing,
Until he opens his heart and soul,
Lower man stumbles through the dark,
Until he discovers his truth through his own glow.

Janine Palmer (Silver Moon)

Dragon's Breath

There she stood on the tiny island,
In the middle of a frozen lake,
The ice was cracking and breaking,
He said he put her there for her own sake.

He was a tyrant, so controlling,
With nefarious rage emanating from his eyes,
As compassionate as her heart was,
It was him she'd grown to despise.

He'd placed her there to think,
About letting go of her need to be strong,
And to come up with better ways to serve him,
It was to him that she belonged.

She told him to go straight to hell,
To stop being so focused on his own needs,
To burn away with transformative fire,
His steadfast lust and greed.

Her velvet gown of crimson red,
Billowed in the frozen breeze,
The softest words of hope and love,
Were whispered through the trees.

They whispered, "Help is coming,
Be wary of what may come,
Don't be surprised by unexpected things,
Be brave oh valiant one."

And what she saw then in the distance,
Was quite a shocking sight,
With mighty wings approaching her,
Silent in its flight.

A glorious mystical blue dragon,
So massive there in the sky,
And as it circled her three times,
It looked her in the eyes.

Surprisingly she felt no fear,
In the presence of this awesome being,
She steadied herself with courage,
In the face of what she was seeing.

The trees were still whispering to her,
She understood every word they said,
They told her what was happening,
The words whirling round her head.

Since she had raised her consciousness,
With her good deeds and good intentions,
She'd gained a level of awareness,
To receive this guide from higher dimensions.

Previously this being was invisible to her,
But it was time for her redemption,
The magnificence of this mystical being,
Commanded every bit of her attention.

She was a holy being on earth,
She was here to do God's deeds,
She was a bringer of the light,
She was a planter of God's seeds.

She was a messenger and a priestess,
She was a warrior and peacemaker as well,
She overflowed with such compassion,
But her compassionate flame could be hell.

Her compassionate flame was an amazing strength,
It was ever her driving force,
She was a healer, a witch and a holy woman,
Which guided her along her course.

She would love you and heal you,
She would guide you and get you through,
But her flame could come out and burn you,
For she had dragon blood in her too.

Her flame came on when injustice raged,
When it was staring her in the face,
She would swiftly correct many a falsehood,
Shedding light to put it in its place.

She would whisper to the angels,
And listen to the gods and the masters speak,
The compassionate love she shared,
Flowed from a holy place so deep.

The dragon alighted before her,
With such other-worldly grace,
Which promptly brought a delighted smile,
To her lovely face.

The presence of the dragon,
Was familiar to her now,
It was something very comforting,
She'd always sensed somehow.

She was meeting an ancient friend,
Who was familiar and yet unknown,
A grin could be seen in the dragon's eyes,
And she knew it was her own.

She reached out her slender hands,
To gently touch its face,
And she knew she was touching something heavenly,
She was touching holy grace.

The dragon's mouth then opened,
And with the slightest puff of smoke,
It whispered to her in Gaelic,
'My Lady, we love you so.'

The dragon bid her to get on its back,
It would take her away to another land,
Where her healing gifts would be honored,
And in her glory she would stand.

Janine Palmer (Silver Moon)

Passion Expressed

She went on a healing journey,
With an intuitive shaman as her guide,
For the purpose of soul retrieval,
To call back pieces of her soul from where they hide.

To heal and release any blocks in her energy,
To reintegrate any missing parts of her soul,
With the help of her guides and higher beings,
To assist her higher purpose for the goal.

Many beings are in divine service,
To God, to Source, to the ALL,
To assist mankind as he stumbles,
And to assist him or her when they fall.

To call back the missing pieces,
Lost or left behind due to trauma and such,
And the feeling which had followed her,
Of something missing so very much.

And into the cave she entered,
Her shaman led the way,
She met the guardian of the lower world,
And the guardian of past lives to heal today.

She offered him a trinket,
A beautiful ring set with turquoise stones,
And he gave her a very special gift,
Before the shaman spoke of the hollow bone.

The guardian bestowed upon her a passionate kiss,
Something missing in her life, cut away by a knife,
It was something her soul so needed,
Which had been taken away by life.

But things are only ever temporary,
And new blessings will always present,
But we must be open to receive them,
Metanoia, to repent and not to resent.

Energy blocks were acknowledged,
And they were healed from a space of love,
With the crow and the raven's powerful energies,
And the energy of the dove.

Her spirit animals were present,
Her guides and her angels were too,
And she opened herself to allow the healing,
And divine love to come right through.

She was advised to make more time for herself,
Because she did so much for others,
She was advised to have more compassion for herself,
As she did for her sisters and brothers.

The healing energies from invitation or intention,
The healing energies from musical instruments and sound,
The healing from and for the heart and soul,
Are ever present and all around.

Janine Palmer (Silver Moon)

Wisps

Wisps of floating clouds revealed at once,
When they cleared, the brightest moon,
And the birds were squawking loudly,
At their beloved goddess's awaited return.

They adored her sweet presence among them,
Her kindness and energy so fair,
How she whispered sweet nothings to all of them,
And her essence and beauty so fair.

She had gone away to meet her warrior,
Her divine masculine connection to balance her soul,
And they could tell by the much improved quality,
And the bright color of her light's full glow.

They were happy to see a smile there,
Emanating from her spirit, her soul and her face,
She was happy, ever so happy,
And it showed profoundly in her grace.

She was a gracious being in so many ways,
Who deserved the love she always bared,
To have her experiences here with him,
For love to be felt and cherished and shared.

A man of strength who would recognize her,
Who would honor her in a masculine way,
To balance each the other,
To love and to laugh and to play.

She shared experiences and wisdom learned,
To bear vulnerability in trust and grace,
To be able to see the effects of creating,
A smile of the deepest happiness upon another's face.

To allow any tears to flow which need release,
To be present with no judgment to be found,
And to be ingratitude for the blessing of the other,
As in balance and flow, new treasures abound.

The wisps of things which guide us,
The wisps of things which flow,
The wisps of blessings and challenges,
And how we open, evolve and grow.

The wisps of healing energy,
On so many levels so many people need,
To be present as a healing force,
To release and let things flow, even if they bleed.

Janine Palmer (Silver Moon)

About the Author

Janine Palmer (Spirit Silver Moon) grew up in Northern California and resides in Utah today. After the devastating county-wide wild fires in Southern California and global economic collapse, Janine and her family endured physical, economical and emotional losses, along with the loss of friendships. Judgmental treatment by so-called religious people (family/friends) caused her to question religions due to poor treatment by others in religious ideology. These initiations tested her inner strength and caused her to investigate more deeply for truth, what brings true happiness, forward movement, the evolvement of the soul and ultimately she discovered her calling.

She was a phoenix who rose from her own ashes with a powerful story to share of truth, strength, wisdom, compassion, love and taking one's power back. We must remember our magnificence to in order to rise above so much illusion. Looking for answers, Janine Palmer (Silver Moon) extensively studied and continues to study multiple healing modalities for emotional and spiritual healing.

Janine has studied World Religions, Spirituality, Early Christianity, Gnosticism, Philosophy, Critical Thinking, Biblical Scholars, and Spiritual teachers. Janine is a Clinical Hypnotherapist and Shamanic Practitioner. In the spiritual and emotional arenas, Janine has studied and become certified in the following areas: Cognitive Behavioral Hypnotherapy, Ericksonian Hypnosis, Energy Psychology, Emotional Freedom Technique (EFT or Tapping), Kinesiology, Muscle Testing,

Neuro-linguistic Programming (NLP) the language of the mind, Reiki Master and Gamma Healing for overcoming energy vampires, healing emotional traumas, anxiety, depression and PTSD, and Shamanic Journey Work.

These modalities are helpful for releasing stress, old pain, resentment, anger, doubt, grief, unforgiveness or anything which blocks forward movement. Through her healing sessions, whether held in person, via phone or skype, she has helped others heal, grow, overcome obstacles and move forward lighter after releasing what no longer serves. This knowledge and wisdom is contained within her writings of uplifting messages for healing. She shares tools we can use to assist ourselves and others on their path. Janine is the author of multiple books containing many genres and messages from various teachings and modalities. The four main genres are story poems, romance, rising above dogma and emotional and spiritual healing. These are presented as poetic tales which have received very positive support and feedback around the world.

Janine's compassion and calling to help others break free of limiting and painful situations can be felt through the writings contained her he book series Divine Heretic. She does God's work for humanity, for the collective and greater good. It is a gift and a blessing she is very grateful for.

www.ingramcontent.com/pod-product-compliance
Lightning Source LLC
Chambersburg PA
CBHW071553080526
44588CB00010B/898